Keyboarding Course

SUSIE H. VANHUSS, PH.D.
University of South Carolina

CONNIE M. FORDE, PH.D.
Mississippi State University

DONNA L. WOO
Cypress College, California

SOUTH-WESTERN
THOMSON LEARNING

Australia · Canada · Mexico · Singapore · Spain · United Kingdom · United States

College Keyboarding: Keyboarding Course, Lessons 1-25
by Susan H. VanHuss, Connie M. Forde, Donna Woo

Team Leader:
Karen Schmohe

Project Manager:
Jane Phelan

Editor:
Martha Conway

Channel Manager:
Chris McNamee

Marketing Coordinator:
Lori Pegg

Consulting Editor:
Diane Durkee

Production Manager:
Tricia Boies

Manufacturing Coordinator:
Charlene Taylor

Design Project Manager:
Stacy Jenkins Shirley

Rights and Permissions Manager:
Linda Ellis

Cover Design:
Paul Neff Design

Cover Image:
©Getty Images/Joseph Drivas

Internal Design:
Grannan Graphic Design Ltd.

Compositor:
D&G Limited, LLC

Printer:
Quebecor World, Dubuque

COPYRIGHT © 2002 South-Western.

South-Western is a division of Thomson Learning, Inc. Thomson Learning™ is a trademark used herein under license.

ISBN: 0-538-72553-2

Printed in the United States of America
1 2 3 4 5 6 7 8 9 0 07 06 05 04 03 02 01

For more information, contact South-Western
5101 Madison Road
Cincinnati, OH 45227-1490

Or you can visit our internet site at www.swep.com.

For permission to use material from this text or product, contact us by
Phone: 1-800-730-2214
Fax: 1-800-730-2215
www.thomsonrights.com

FAMILY OF PRODUCTS

Texts

Keyboarding Course (Lessons 1-25) – Lessons cover alphabetic, numeric, and symbol keys, and skillbuilding. Combined with *Keyboarding Pro* software, you have a system that guarantees a strong keyboarding foundation.

Keyboarding and Word Processing (Lessons 1-60) – Develop marketable skills with this all-in-one keyboarding, formatting, and word processing text. Formats include business letters, standard memos, reports, tables, and newsletters with graphics. Microsoft Certified: Core Level.

Advanced Word Processing (Lessons 61-120) – Advances students to the expert level of word processing as they master document design. Microsoft Certified: Expert Level.

Keyboarding and Word Processing, Complete Course, (Lessons 1-120) – Students progress from that of a beginner to an expert user without having to change texts. Microsoft Certified: Core and Expert Levels.

Integrated Applications – Combines instruction on all Microsoft Office XP tools. Microsoft Certified: Core Level.

Microsoft Word Applications – Project-based instruction that reinforces word processing, document design, Internet research, and communication skills. Reviews both Core and Expert level skills.

Instructor's Manual/Key – Available for both Lessons 1-60 and 61-120. Traditional printed format.

Technology Solutions

Keyboarding Pro, Ver. 3 – Covers alphabetic, numeric, keypad, and skillbuilding instruction. Excellent instruction for learning and reviewing keyboarding. Student version available.

CheckPro 2002 – Assessment software that provides immediate feedback on keyboarding and proofreading skills. Checks drills, timings, selected documents, and production assessments for speed and accuracy. Student version available.

WebTutor for College Keyboarding 15E – Online supplement that includes multimedia activities, Web links, presentations, quizzes, flashcards, enrichment materials, model documents, and more for each text. Available for WebCT or Blackboard.

MicroPace Pro – Timed writing, paced skill development, drills, and error diagnostics software. Correlates with *College Keyboarding, 15E.* Student version available.

KeyChamp – Unique program that develops speed by analyzing a student's two-stroke key combinations and providing drills that build speed on slow key combinations.

Instructor CD – Solutions, data files, teaching tips, and objective and performance assessments, Keyboarding Pro User's Manual, and more—all in an easy-to-use format.

www.collegekeyboarding.com

iii

PREFACE

COLLEGE KEYBOARDING, KEYBOARDING COURSE is a learning package designed to prepare you for the career of your choice. This ultra-successful learning package combines *Windows 2000*, state-of-the-art operating system; *KEYBOARDING PRO*, a very effective all-in-one keyboarding instruction program; and well-written learning materials presented in an easy-to-learn format. This winning combination ensures that you will have marketable skills regardless of the career you choose.

Career Skills

Pick your career—manager, engineer, scientist, physician, attorney, administrative employee, educator, sales executive, accountant, computer specialist, factory worker, or any one of a host of other choices. The critical skills for success are the ability to access and manage knowledge and to communicate effectively. Knowledge management and communication tools include keyboarding, word processing, Internet usage, and the other software applications. *College Keyboarding* will enable you to master these knowledge management and communication skills required in virtually every profession.

Keyboarding Skill

Keyboarding is the foundation skill required for effective computer usage. As with the development of any high-level skill, you must consistently use proper techniques and meaningful practice. By the end of this course, you will be able to:

- Key the letters, numbers, symbols, and numeric keypad by touch.
- Key straight copy for 3' at 25–30 gross words a minute (*gwam*) with good accuracy.
- Develop proofreading and editing skills.

Keyboarding Software

Learning to type properly has never been more important...and more fun. *Keyboarding Pro* software consists of four modules that cover the alphabet and punctuation keys, top-row numbers and symbols, the numeric keypad, and a Skill Builder module that will boost your speed and accuracy. Challenging games, along with progress graphs, interactive videos, 3-D models to view proper posture and hand positions, and a full-featured word processor, will keep you motivated.

A student version of *Keyboarding Pro* is also available. You can install this version on your home computer and use it long after your class is over to continue to build your skills.

Communication, Internet, and Word Processing Skills

Of course, the real purpose of keyboarding is to use the computer as a writing and communication tool. The *Keyboarding Course* also includes extra activities that provide training in these areas:

- Data entry practice for the numeric keypad (completed in the Open Screen of Numeric Keypad).
- Communication skills (capitalization, number expression, subject/verb agreement, etc.).
- Internet basics (browser, e-mail, and search engine).
- Word processing basics, including guidelines for formatting business letters and a basic unbound report. All word processing activities will be completed in the Open Screen of *Keyboarding Pro*.

No matter what career you pursue, you will have the necessary keyboarding skills you need after completing the *Keyboarding Course*. And you will join the 75 million people who have learned to type from South-Western, the proven leader in keyboarding education.

TABLE OF CONTENTS

Make a Lasting Impression
with Key Features from College Keyboarding 15E

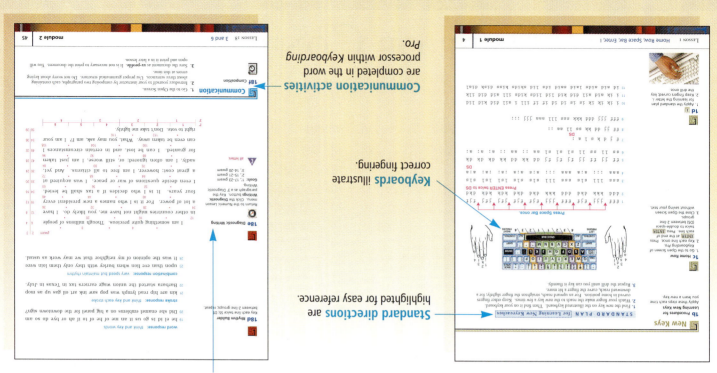

Communication activities are completed in the word processor within Keyboarding Pro.

Keyboards illustrate correct fingering.

Standard directions are highlighted for easy reference.

A diagnostic report of errors on timed writings is available.

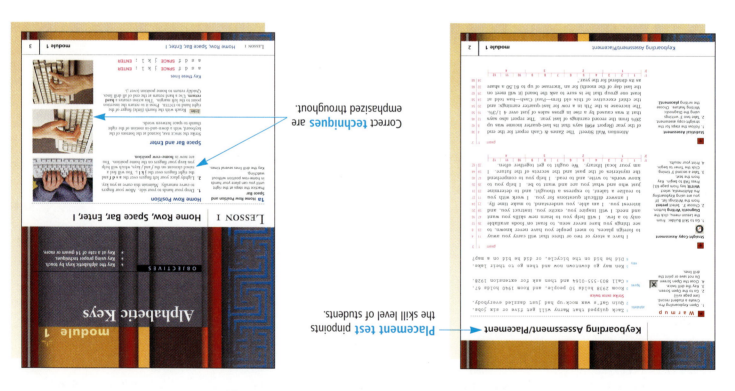

Correct techniques are emphasized throughout.

Placement test pinpoints the skill level of students.

KNOW YOUR COMPUTER

The numbered parts are found on most computers. The location of some parts will vary.

1. **CPU (Central Processing Unit)**: Internal operating unit or "brain" of computer.

2. **Disk drive**: Reads data from and writes data to a disk.

3. **Monitor**: Displays text and graphics on a screen.

4. **Mouse**: Used to input commands.

5. **Keyboard**: An arrangement of letter, figure, symbol, control, function, and editing keys and a numeric keypad.

Keyboard Arrangement

1. **Alphanumeric keys**: Letters, numbers, and symbols.

2. **Numeric keypad**: Keys at the right side of the keyboard used to enter numeric copy and perform calculations.

3. **Function (F) keys**: Used to execute commands, sometimes with other keys. Commands vary with software.

4. **Arrow keys**: Move insertion point up, down, left, or right.

5. **ESC (Escape)**: Closes a software menu or dialog box.

6. **TAB**: Moves the insertion point to a preset position.

7. **CAPS LOCK**: Used to make all capital letters.

8. **SHIFT**: Makes capital letters and symbols shown at tops of number keys.

9. **CTRL (Control)**: With other key(s), executes commands. Commands may vary with software.

10. **ALT (Alternate)**: With other key(s), executes commands. Commands may vary with software.

11. **Space Bar**: Inserts a space in text.

12. **ENTER (RETURN)**: Moves insertion point to margin and down to next line. Also used to execute commands.

13. **DELETE**: Removes text to the right of insertion point.

14. **NUM LOCK**: Activates/deactivates numeric keypad.

15. **INSERT**: Activates insert or typeover.

16. **BACKSPACE**: Deletes text to the left of insertion point.

WELCOME TO WINDOWS®

Microsoft® *Windows*® is an **operating system,** a program that manages all other software applications on your computer and its peripherals such as the mouse and printer. Software applications that run under *Windows* have many common features. Depending on the version of your operating system, some features may look, work, or be named slightly differently on your computer.

The Desktop

When your computer is turned on and ready to use, it will display a **desktop,** the main working area. The illustration shows a *Windows*® *2000* desktop. Your desktop will have many of the same features. Depending on what programs are on your computer and how the desktop has been arranged, it may look different.

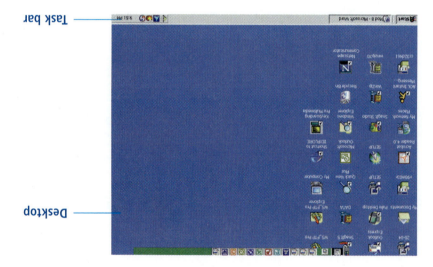
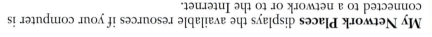

Desktop

Task bar

The desktop displays icons and a taskbar. **Icons** provide an easy way to access programs and documents that you use frequently. Note three icons in particular:

My Computer displays the disk drives, CD-ROM drives, and printers that are attached to your computer.

My Network Places displays the available resources if your computer is connected to a network or to the Internet.

Recycle Bin stores files and folders that have been deleted from the hard drive. Documents in the Recycle Bin may be restored and returned to their folders. However, once you empty the Recycle Bin, the documents are deleted and cannot be restored.

The bar at the bottom of the desktop is the taskbar. The **taskbar** displays the Start button on the left, a button for each program or document that is open, and the system clock on the right (your taskbar may have additional icons). The taskbar enables you to open programs and navigate on your computer.

The Start Button

 The **Start button** opens the Start menu, which lists a variety of items from which to choose such as programs and documents.

The Start menu is divided into three sections.

The *top* section contains applications or shortcuts you may have added to your computer such as an antivirus program.

The *center* section contains a list of options such as Programs, Documents, Search, and Help.

The *lower* section contains basic commands such as Log On/Off and Shut Down.

To open an item listed on the Start menu, point to the item and click the left mouse button. A right arrow beside a menu item indicates that a cascading or submenu with more options is available for that item. (*Note:* If an icon is displayed on the desktop, you can double-click the icon to open the program, document, or folder that it represents.)

The Mouse

Windows requires the use of a mouse or other pointing device such as a touch pad built into your keyboard. A mouse has two buttons. The left button is used to select text or commands, to open files or menus, or to drag objects. The right button is used to display shortcut menus.

To move the pointer, you must move the mouse. If you have a touch pad on your keyboard, move the pointer by moving your finger on the touch pad. The mouse or touch pad is used to perform four basic actions:

Point: Move the mouse so that the pointer touches something displayed onscreen.

Click: Point to an item, quickly press the mouse button once, and release it.

Double-click: Point to an item; quickly press the mouse button twice, and release it.

Drag: Point to an item, then hold down the mouse button while you move the mouse to reposition the item.

The mouse pointer changes in appearance depending on its location on the desktop and the task being performed.

The *vertical blinking bar* indicates the current position of the cursor.

The *I-beam* indicates the location of the mouse pointer. To reposition the cursor at this point, you must click the mouse button.

The *arrow* indicates that you can select items. It displays when the mouse is located outside the text area. You can point to a toolbar icon to display the function of that icon.

The *hourglass* indicates that *Windows* is processing a command.

A *double-headed arrow* appears when the pointer is at the border of a window; it is used to change the size.

Windows Features

Windows displays folders, applications, and individual documents in windows. A **window** is a work area on the desktop that can be resized or moved. To resize a window, point to the border. When the pointer changes to a double-headed arrow, drag the window to the desired size. To move a window, point to the title bar, drag it to the new position, and release the mouse button.

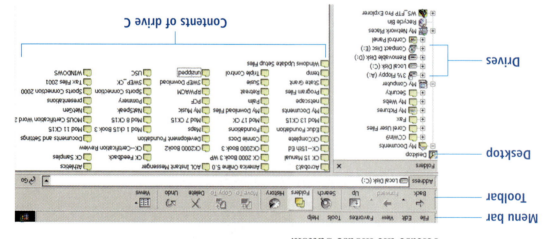

Menu bar

Toolbar

Desktop

Drives

Folders

Contents of drive C

The basic features of all windows are the same. Each window contains the following:

Title bar: Displays the name of the application that is currently open and the path (folder name). The Title bar also includes several buttons at the right.

Minimize button: Reduces the window to a button on the taskbar. To restore the window, click the button on the taskbar.

Maximize button: Enlarges a window to full-screen size.

Restore button: When you maximize a window, the Maximize button is replaced with a Restore button that, when clicked, returns the window to its original size.

Close button: Closes the application.

Minimize **Maximize** **Close** **Restore**

Menu bar: Displays commands available in the software.

Toolbars: Display icons that offer a convenient way to access frequently used commands. Applications programs often have different toolbars for different tasks.

Scroll bars: Enable you to see material that does not fit on one screen. You can click the arrows on the scroll bars or drag the scroll box to move through a document.

Help

Help is available for *Windows*. Help is also available with each software application that you use. Generally you will use the Help feature provided with the application. To access *Windows* Help, click the Start button, and then click Help. A list of topics will be displayed. From the list, choose the appropriate one by highlighting the topic and clicking on it.

You can also click **Index** to display a list of specific items in alphabetical order. As you key the characters of the topic in the entry box, the program automatically moves to items beginning with the keyed letters. When the correct topic is displayed, highlight it and choose display. If you prefer, you can scroll through the list of topics until you find what you are looking for.

To search for a topic, key the topic in the Search box and press ENTER to see a display of Help pages that contain the topic. Select the topic and click **Display** to present the information.

Shut Down

Before you exit *Windows*, be sure that all programs have been closed. To exit *Windows*, click the **Start** button, and then click **Shut Down** to display the Shut Down dialog box. Check to be sure Shut down is displayed, and then click **OK**. If Shut down is not displayed, click the down arrow at the right, then select **Shut down**. Never just turn your computer off. Windows may notify you when the computer can be turned off, or it may automatically shut down once you click OK. This will vary depending upon how your computer was set up.

FILE MANAGEMENT

As with paper files, it is important to establish a logical and easy-to-use computer file management system to organize your files efficiently so that you can find them quickly and easily. You can manage files from the desktop or from My Computer or Windows Explorer.

Understand the File System

Computer files are stored on **disks** specified by their location. The desktop of the computer in the example below has a hard disk drive (C), a floppy disk drive (A), a removable drive (D), and a CD-ROM drive (E). Drives are illustrated and named.

Drives on the computer

View Contents of a Drive

To view the contents of a drive:

- Click the **My Computer** icon on the desktop.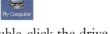

- When the drives display in the first column, double-click the drive you want to see. Note in the Address box below that Drive A is displayed. The folders contained in Drive A are displayed in the right half of the screen.

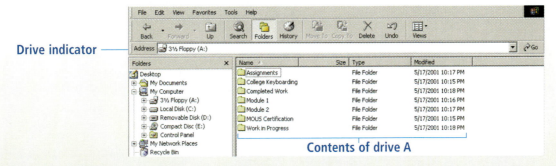

Drive indicator

Contents of drive A

Working with Folders and Files

View Contents of a Folder

Folders are listed in alphabetic order. (In the illustration, Assignments is listed first.) To see the contents of a folder, double-click the folder. Folders may contain files, other programs, and folders. (*Note:* You can also use Windows Explorer to view a hierarchal list of files on your computer by clicking Start, pointing to Programs, pointing to Accessories, and clicking Windows Explorer.)

View Data and Arrange Files

Files and folders within My Computer can be viewed in different ways: as Large Icons, Small Icons, List, or Details. In the illustration above, items are shown in List view.

To change the view, click **View** on the menu; then choose a view. You may want to experiment with each of the views to decide which one you prefer.

Folders are usually listed in alphabetical order. You can also arrange them in descending order by date, size, or type of file. To rearrange the order of files or folders, select **Details** from the View menu, and then click on one of headings displayed above the files or folders such as size, date, or type.

Folders are extremely important in managing files. You will want to create folders to organize and store related files or other folders. You can do so using My Computer on the desktop or Windows Explorer. *Note:* If you are using only *Keyboarding Pro* software, it is not necessary to create additional folders.

Create Folder

To create a folder, click **My Computer**; then double-click the drive or folder that will contain the new folder. (Drive A has been selected in the example.) In the window that opens, from the menu bar, click **File**, point to **New**, and click **Folder**. Select and replace **New Folder** with the folder name you want.

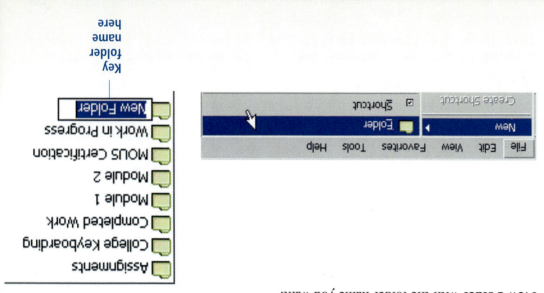

Key folder name here

Name Files and Folders

Good file organization begins with giving your folders and files names that are logical and easy to understand. In the example, the user created a folder on Drive A for Completed Work and a second folder for Work in Progress.

Rename Files and Folders

Occasionally, you may want to rename a file or folder. To do so, right-click the file or folder, choose **Rename**, key the new name, and press ENTER. You can also rename files using the Windows Explorer menu.

Move and Copy Files and Folders

To move files or folders, double-click My Computer on the desktop. Double-click the drive that contains the file or folder you want to move, and then locate the item. Be sure the place you want to move the file or folder to is visible. Press and hold down the left mouse button and drag the pointer to the new location.

To copy a file or folder, press and hold down CTRL while you drag.

Note: If you drag a file or folder to a location on the same disk, it will be moved. If you drag an item to a different disk, it will be copied. To move the item, press and hold down SHIFT while dragging.

When you are moving or copying items, selecting (clicking) several items at once can save time. To select consecutive items, click the fist item, hold down SHIFT, and click the last item. To select items in different places, hold down CRTL while you click each item.

Delete Files and Folders

You can select and delete several files and folders at once, just as you can select several items to move or copy. If you delete a folder, you automatically delete any files and folders inside it.

To delete a file or folder and send it to the Recycle Bin, right-click on the file or folder, and choose **Delete**. Answer **Yes** to the question about sending the item to the Recycle Bin. (*Note:* You can also delete files and folders using Windows Explorer.)

Restore Deleted Files and Folders

When you delete a file or folder, the item goes to the Recycle Bin. If you have not emptied the Recycle Bin, you can restore files and folders stored there.

- Minimize the working window, and then double-click the Recycle Bin on the desktop to open the Recycle Bin window.
- Select the file you want to restore, right-click to display the shortcut menu, and choose **Restore**. You can also choose **Restore** from the File menu.

Close the Recycle Bin window. Click the folder where the file was originally located, and it should now be restored.

WELCOME TO KEYBOARDING PRO

Keyboarding Pro combines the latest technology with South-Western's superior method for teaching keyboarding. The Alphabetic and Numeric and Skill modules of *Keyboarding Pro* or *Keyboarding Pro Multimedia*, correspond to Lessons 1–25 in *College Keyboarding*. Use Skill Builder to boost your speed and accuracy after you learn the alphabetic keys. Use the Numeric Keypad to learn the keypad by touch.

Getting Started

1. Click the **Start** button and then select **Programs**. Select the South-Western Keyboarding program group and click **Keyboarding Pro**. If you chose to add an icon to your desktop during the install, you may also double-click on the icon to start the program.

2. Click anywhere on the splash screen to remove it and bring up the Log In dialog box.

The first time you use *Keyboarding Pro*, you must enter your user information and indicate where you will store your data. This process creates a student record. You will create a student record **only once** so that the results of all lessons are stored in one file.

1. From the Log In dialog box, click **New User**.

2. Enter your name (first name then last name), your Class ID, and a password. Write down the password and store it in a safe place. You will need to use this password each time you enter the program.

3. Specify the data location. The default storage path is **c:\Program Files\Keyboarding Pro\Students**. If you will be storing on Drive A or if you have a student subdirectory on the network, set the path accordingly. Click the **Folder** icon to change the page to Drive A or browse to locate your network folder.

Main Menu

The Main menu displays after you have logged in. Note these special features. Other features will be explained as you move through the program.

Open Screen is a word processor with a timer. You can practice your keyboarding or take a timed writing.

Animations demonstrate proper posture and hand positions. Review techniques frequently.

Quick Review includes numerous keyboarding drills for improving techniques and keyboarding skill.

Diagnostic Writings are timed writings (1', 3', or 5') with extensive error analysis. They are accessed from the Lesson menus of Numeric and Skill Builder. Writings are keyed from the textbook.

4. If desired, click the **Preferences** button and update the information. Click **OK** to complete the registration.

Each time you enter *Keyboarding Pro* after the first time, the Log In dialog box displays. Click your name and enter your password. If you do not see your name, click **Locate** to locate the drive where your student record is located (Drive A or your folder on the network.)

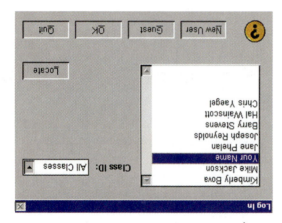

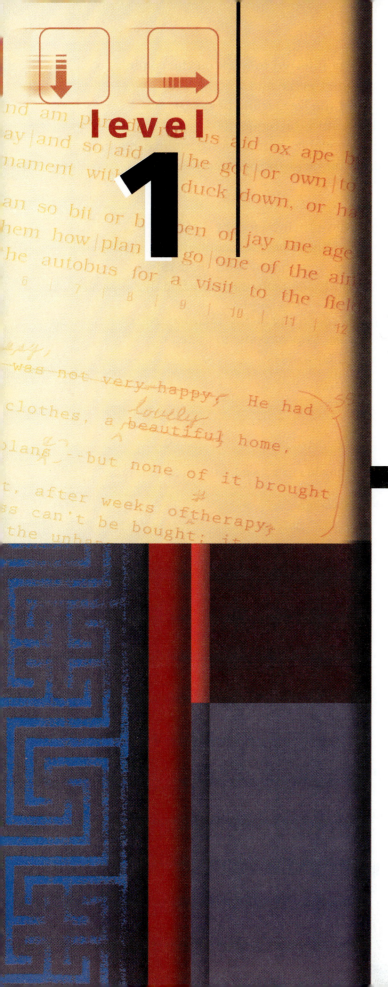

level
1

Developing Keyboarding Skill

KEYBOARDING

To key the alphabetic and number keys by touch with good technique.

To key approximately 25 *wam* with good accuracy.

COMMUNICATION SKILLS

To apply proofreaders' marks and revise text.

To create simple documents in a basic word processor.

Drill 1

Key the sentences, correcting the errors in pronoun case. Save as **pronoun-drill1.**

1. Marie and me have volunteered to work on the committee.
2. Give the assignment to George and I.
3. It is she who received the free airline ticket.
4. It was not me who sent in the request.
5. She has more time available than me for handling this project.
6. Did you see Cheryl and he at the opening session?

Drill 2

Key the sentences, correcting the errors in pronoun and antecedent agreement. Save as **pronoun-drill2.**

1. Each student must have their own data disk.
2. Several students have his or her own computer.
3. Some of the employees were happy with their raises.
4. The company has not decided whether they will make profit sharing available.
5. All candidates must submit his or her résumé. (*To key the acute accent mark, press* CTRL + *apostrophe; then key* **e**.)
6. Napoleon organized their armies.

 Apostrophe Guides

Apostrophes

1. Add 's to a singular noun not ending in *s.*

2. Add 's to a singular noun not ending in *s* or *z* sound if the ending *s* is pronounced as a syllable.
   Sis's lunch, Russ's car, Buzz's average

3. Add ' only if the ending *s* or *z* is awkward to pronounce.
   series' outcome, ladies' shoes, Delibes' music, Cortez' quest

4. Add 's to a plural noun that does not end in *s.*
   men's notions, children's toys, mice's tracks

5. Add only ' after a plural noun ending in *s.*
   horses' hooves, lamps' shades

6. Add 's after the last noun in a series to show joint possession of two or more people.
   Jack and Judy's house; Peter, Paul, and Mary's song

7. Add 's to each noun to show individual possession of two or more persons.
   Li's and Ted's tools, Jill's and Ed's races.

Drill 3

Key the sentences, correcting all errors in apostrophes. DS between items. Save as **apostrophes-drill3.**

1. Mary Thomas, my neighbors sister, will take care of my son.
2. The assistant gave him the instructors telephone number.
3. The announcers microphone is never shut off.
4. His father-in-laws home will be open for touring next week.
5. Two hours time is not sufficient to set up the exhibit.
6. Someones car lights have been left on.

Keyboarding Assessment/Placement

 W a r m u p

1. Open *Keyboarding Pro*. Create a student record. (see page xviii)
2. Go to the Open Screen.
3. Key the drill twice.
4. Close the Open Screen. Do not save or print the drill lines.

alphabetic
1 Zack quipped that Marny will get five or six jobs.
2 Quin Gaf's wax mock-up had just dazzled everybody.
Strike ENTER twice

figures
3 Room 2938 holds 50 people, and Room 1940 holds 67.
4 Call 803-555-0164 and then ask for extension 1928.

easy
5 Ken may go downtown now and then go to their lake.
6 Did he bid on the bicycle, or did he bid on a map?

gwam 1' | 3'

 Straight-Copy Assessment

1. Go to Skill Builder. From the Lesson menu, click the **Diagnostic Writing** button.
2. Choose 3'. Select **pretest** from the Writings list. (If you are using *Keyboarding Pro Multimedia*, select **Writ10**; key from page 63.) Press TAB to begin. Key from the text.
3. Take a second 3' timing. Click the Timer to begin.
4. Print your results.

	1'	3'
I have a story or two or three that will carry you away | 11 | 4 |
to foreign places, to meet people you have never known, to | 23 | 8 |
see things you have never seen, to feast on foods available | 35 | 12 |
only to a few. I will help you to learn new skills you want | 47 | 16 |
and need; I will inspire you, excite you, instruct you, and | 59 | 20 |
interest you. I am able, you understand, to make time fly. | 71 | 24 |

I answer difficult questions for you. I work with you | 11 | 27 |
to realize a talent, to express a thought, and to determine | 23 | 31 |
just who and what you are and want to be. I help you to | 35 | 35 |
know words, to write, and to read. I help you to comprehend | 47 | 40 |
the mysteries of the past and the secrets of the future. I | 59 | 44 |
am your local library. We ought to get together often. | 70 | 47 |

```
1' | 1 | 2 | 3 | 4 | 5 | 6 | 7 | 8 | 9 | 10 | 11 | 12 |
3' |     1     |       2      |       3      |      4       |
```

gwam 1' | 3'

 Statistical Assessment

1. Follow the steps for the straight-copy assessment.
2. Take two 3' writings using the Diagnostic Writing feature. Choose the writing **placement2**.

	1'	3'
Attention Wall Street! The Zanes & Cash report for the end | 4 | 38 |
of the year (Report #98) says that its last-quarter income was up | 8 | 42 |
26% from the record earnings of last year. The report also says | 12 | 46 |
that it was caused by a rise in gross sales of just over 4 1/3%. | 16 | 50 |
The increase is the 7th in a row for last-quarter earnings; and | 20 | 54 |
the chief executive of this old firm—Paul Cash—has told at | 24 | 58 |
least one group that he is sure to ask the board (it will meet on | 28 | 62 |
the last day of the month) for an "increase of up to $1.50 a share | 32 | 66 |
as its dividend for the year." | 34 | 68 |

```
1' | 1 | 2 | 3 | 4 | 5 | 6 | 7 | 8 | 9 | 10 | 11 | 12 |
3' |     1     |       2      |       3      |      4       |
```

COMMUNICATION SKILLS 3

Pronoun Guides

Pronoun Case

Use the **nominative case** (*I, you, we, she, he, they, it, who*):

1. When the pronoun acts as the **subject of a verb**.

   Jim and *I* went to the movies.

   Mike and *she* were best friends.

2. When the pronoun is used as a **predicate pronoun**. (The verb *be* is a linking verb; it links the noun/pronoun to the predicate.)

   It was *she* who answered the phone.

   The person who objected was *I*.

Use the **objective case** (*me, you, us, her, him, them, it, whom*):

3. When the pronoun is used as a **direct** or **indirect object**.

   Jill invited *us* to the meeting.

   The printer gave Bill and *me* tickets to the game.

4. When the pronoun is an **object of the preposition**.

   I am going with **you** and **him**.

   This issue is between **you** and **me**.

Pronoun-Antecedent Agreement

1. The **antecedent** is the word in the sentence that the pronoun refers to. In the examples, the antecedent is bold and the pronoun is in italics.

   Players must show *their* birth certificates.

   The *boy* lost **his** wallet.

2. The antecedent must agree with the pronoun in **person** (first, second, third).

   I am pleased that *my* project placed first. (Both are first person.)

   You must stand by *your* display at the science fair. (Both are second person.)

   The ash **tree** has lost *its* leaves. (Both are third person.)

3. The antecedent must agree with the pronoun in **gender** (neuter when gender of antecedent is unknown).

   Gail said that *she* preferred the duplex apartment.

   The adjustable **chair** sits firmly on *its* five-leg base.

   The **dog** looked for *its* master for days.

4. The antecedent must agree with the pronoun in **number**. If the antecedent of a pronoun is singular, use a singular pronoun. If the antecedent is plural, use a plural pronoun.

   All **members** of the class paid *their* dues.

   Each of the Girl Scouts brought **her** sleeping bag.

Alphabetic Keys

OBJECTIVES

✳ Key the alphabetic keys by touch.
✳ Key using proper techniques.
✳ Key at a rate of 14 *gwam* or more.

LESSON 1 | Home Row, Space Bar, Enter, I

1a Home Row Position and Space Bar

Practice the steps at the right until you can place your hands in home-row position without watching.

Key the drill lines several times.

Home Row Position

1. Drop your hands to your side. Allow your fingers to curve naturally. Maintain this curve as you key.

2. Lightly place your left fingers over the **a s d f** and the right fingers over the **j k l ;**. You will feel a raised element on the *f* and *j* keys, which will help you keep your fingers on the home position. You are now in **home–row position**.

Space Bar and Enter

Strike the SPACE BAR, located at the bottom of the keyboard, with a down-and-in motion of the right thumb to space between words.

`Enter` Reach with the fourth (little) finger of the right hand to ENTER. Press it to return the insertion point to the left margin. This action creates a **hard return**. Use a hard return at the end of all drill lines. Quickly return to home position (over ;).

Key these lines

a s d f **SPACE** j k l ; **ENTER**
a s d f **SPACE** j k l ; **ENTER**

Drill 1

SUBJECT-VERB AGREEMENT

Review the rules on the previous page, especially Rules 2 and 8 that refer to indefinite pronouns. Key the eight sentences at the right, choosing the correct verb.

1. Everything in the packages (is/are) securely wrapped.
2. None of the mountains (is/are) visible today.
3. Many of the drivers (is/are) following too closely.
4. Everyone (is/are) expected to attend the seminar.
5. Each of the managers (has/have) given us approval.
6. All of the candidates (was/were) invited to the debate.
7. Nobody (want/wants) to be left behind.
8. Few of the animals (is/are) outside today.

Drill 2

SUBJECT-VERB AGREEMENT

Compose and key four sentences, two illustrating each Rule 2 and Rule 8 on the previous page.

Drill 3

SUBJECT/VERB AND CAPITALIZATION

1. Key the ten sentences at the right, choosing the correct verb and applying correct capitalization.

2. Save as **subjectverb-drill3** and print.

1. both of the curies (was/were) nobel prize winners.
2. each of the directors in the sales department (has/have) given us approval.
3. mr. and mrs. thomas funderburk, jr. (was/were) married on november 23, 1936.
4. my sister and her college roommates (plan/plans) to tour london and paris this summer.
5. our new information manager (suggest/suggests) the following salutation when using an attention line: ladies and gentlemen.
6. the body language expert (place/places) his hand on his cheek as he says, "touch your hand to your chin."
7. the japanese child (enjoy/enjoys) the american food her hosts (serve/serves) her.
8. all of the candidates (was/were) invited to the debate at boston college.
9. the final exam (cover/covers) chapters 1-5.
10. turn south onto interstate 20; then take exit 56 to bossier city.

Drill 4

EDITING SKILLS

Key the paragraph. Correct all errors in grammar and capitalization. Save as **editing-drill4**.

This past week I visited the facilities of the magnolia conference center in isle of palms, south carolina, as you requested. bob bremmerton, group manager, was my host for the visit.

magnolia offers many advantages for our leadership training conference. The prices are reasonable; the facilities is excellent; the location is suitable. In addition to the beachfront location, tennis and golf packages are part of the group price.

New Keys

1b Procedures for Learning New Keys

Apply these steps each time you learn a new key.

STANDARD PLAN for Learning New Keyreaches

1. Find the new key on the illustrated keyboard. Then find it on your keyboard.
2. Watch your finger make the reach to the new key a few times. Keep other fingers curved in home position. For an upward reach, straighten the finger slightly; for a downward reach, curve the finger a bit more.
3. Repeat the drill until you can key it fluently.

1c Home Row

1. Go to the Open Screen of *Keyboarding Pro*.
2. Key each line once. Press ENTER at the end of each line. Press ENTER twice to double-space (DS) between 2-line groups.
3. Close the Open Screen without saving your text.

Press Space Bar once.

```
 1  f f f   j j j   f j f   f f f   j j j   f j f   f j f   j f j   j f j   f j f
 2  d d d   k k k   d k d   d d d   k k k   d k d   d k d   k d k   k d k   d k d
```
Press ENTER twice to DS
```
 3  s s s   l l l   s l s   s s s   l l l   s l s   s l s   l s l   l s l   s l s
 4  a a a   ; ; ;   a ; a   a a a   ; ; ;   a ; s   a ; a   ; a ;   ; a ;   a ; a
```
DS
```
 5  f f   j j   f f   j j   f j   f j   f j   d d   k k   d d   k k   d k   d k   d k
 6  s s   l l   s s   l l   s l   s l   s l   a a   ; ;   a a   ; ;   a ;   a ;   a ;
```
```
 7  f  j  d  k  s  l  a  ;
```
DS
```
 8  f f   j j   d d   k k   s s   l l   a a   ; ;
```
```
 9  f f f   j j j   d d d   k k k   s s s   l l l   a a a   j j j   ; ; ;
```

 1d i

1. Apply the standard plan for learning the letter *i*.
2. Keep fingers curved; key the drill once.

```
10  i  ik  ik  ik  is  is  id  id  if  if  ill  i  ail  did  kid  lid
11  i  ik  aid  ail  did  kid  lid  lids  kids  ill  aid  did  ilk
12  id  aid  aids  laid  said  ids  lid  skids  kiss  disk  dial
```

COMMUNICATION SKILLS 2

 **Subject/Verb Agreement**

Use a singular verb

1. With a **singular subject**. (The singular forms of *to be* include: am, is, was. Common errors with *to be* are: you was, we was, they was.)

> She monitors employee morale.
> You are a very energetic worker.
> A split keyboard is in great demand.

2. With most **indefinite pronouns**: *another, anybody, anything, everything, each, either, neither, one, everyone, anyone, nobody*.

> Each of the candidates has raised a considerable amount of money.
> Everyone is eager to read the author's newest novel.
> Neither of the boys is able to attend.

3. With singular subjects joined by *or/nor, either/or, neither/nor*.

> Neither your grammar nor punctuation is correct.
> Either Jody or Jan has your favorite CD.
> John or Connie has volunteered to chaperone the field trip.

4. With a **collective noun** (*family, choir, herd, faculty, jury, committee*) that acts as one unit.

> The jury has reached a decision.
> The council is in an emergency session.
> But:
> The faculty have their assignments. (Each has his/her own assignments.)

5. With words or phrases that express **periods of time, weights, measurements**, or **amounts of money**.

> Fifteen dollars is what he earned.
> Two-thirds of the money has been submitted to the treasurer.
> One hundred pounds is too much.

Use a plural verb

6. With a **plural subject**.

> The students sell computer supplies for their annual fundraiser.
> They are among the top-ranked teams in the nation.

7. With **compound (two or more) subjects** joined by *and*.

> Headaches and backaches are common worker complaints.
> Hard work and determination were two qualities listed by the references.

8. With *some, all, most, none, several, few, both, many*, and *any* when they refer to more than one of the items.

> All of my friends have seen the movie.
> Some of the teams have won two or more games.

1e **Lesson 1 from Software**

1. Read the information at the right. Then do Lesson 1 from *Keyboarding Pro.*

1. Select a lesson from Alphabetic by clicking the lesson number. (Figure 1-1)
2. The first activity is displayed automatically. In Figure 1-2, *Learn Home Row* is in yellow because this activity is active. Follow the directions on screen. Key from the screen.

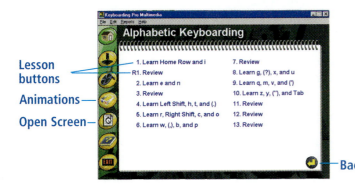

Figure 1-1 Alphabetic Keyboarding Lesson Menu

Figure 1-2 Alphabetic Keyboarding (Lesson 1: Learn Home Row and i)

3. Key the Textbook Keying activity from your textbook (lines 13–18 below). Press ESC to continue.
4. Figure 1-3 shows the Lesson Report. A check mark opposite an exercise indicates that the exercise has been completed.
5. At the bottom, click the **Print** button to print your Lesson Report. Click the **Graph** button to view the Performance Graph.
6. Click the **Back** button twice to return to the Main menu. Then click the **Exit** button to quit the program. Remove your storage disk if necessary. Clean up the work area.

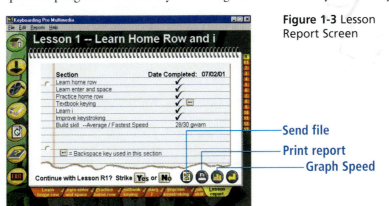

Figure 1-3 Lesson Report Screen

Textbook Keying

2. Key the lines at the right in Textbook Keying. Key each line once. Strike ENTER at the end of each line.
3. When you complete the lesson, print your Lesson Report (step 5 above) and exit the software.

```
13  a  a;  al  ak  aj  s  s;  sl  sk  sj  d  d;  dl  dk  dj

14  j  ja  js  jd  jf  k  ka  ks  kd  kf  l  la  ls  ld  lf

15  a;  sl  a;sl  dkfj  a;sl  dkfj  a;sldkfj  asdf  jk

16  a;  sl  a;sl  dk  fj  dkfj  a;sl  dkfj  fkds;a;  fj

17  f  ff  j  jj  d  dd  k  kk  s  ss  l  ll  a  aa  ;  ;;  fj

18  afj;  a  s  d  f  j  k  l  ;  asdf  jkl;  fdsa  jkl;
```

Drill 1

CAPITALIZATION

Review the rules and examples on the previous page. Then key the sentences, correcting all capitalization errors. Number each item and DS between items. Save as **capitalize-drill 1.**

1. according to one study, the largest ethnic minority group online is hispanics.

2. the american author mark twain said, "always do right; this will gratify some people and astonish the rest."

3. the grand canyon was formed by the colorado river cutting into the high-plateau region of northwestern arizona.

4. the president of russia is elected by popular vote.

5. the hubble space telescope is a cooperative project of the european space agency and the national aeronautics and space administration.

6. the train left north station at 6:45 this morning.

7. the trademark cyberprivacy prevention act would make it illegal for individuals to purchase domains solely for resale and profit.

8. consumers spent $7 billion online between november 1 and december 31, 2000, compared to $3.1 billion for the same period in 1999.

9. new students should attend an orientation session on wednesday, august 15, at 8 a.m. in room 252 of the perry building.

10. the summer book list includes *where the red fern grows* and *the mystery of the missing baseball*.

Drill 2

COMPOSITION

Double-space the paragraph, inserting a proper noun in each blank and applying correct capitalization and number expression.

last _____ , my friend _____ and I had a holiday, so we decided to make the most of our day and take a bicycle trip to _____. before leaving, we stopped at _____ to purchase some high-energy foods to sustain us on our trip. we packed our saddle bags and left about _____ o'clock, traveling _direction_ on _____ street. although we were not on a sightseeing trip, we did pass _____ and _____. by _____ p.m., we returned home exhausted from our journey of _____ miles.

LESSON 1R | Review

✳ Warmup

1Ra Review home row

1. Open *Keyboarding Pro* software.
2. Click the ↓ next to *Class ID* and select your section. Click your name.
3. Key your password and click **OK**.
4. Go to *Lesson R1*.

Key each exercise as directed. Repeat if desired.

Fingers curved and upright

LEFT FINGERS 4 \ 3 \ 2 \ 1 \ 1 / 2 / 3 / 4 RIGHT FINGERS

```
1  f  j  fjf  jj  fj  fj  jf  dd  kk  dd  kk  dk  dk  dk
2  s  ;  s;s  ;;  s;  s;  s;  aa  ;;  aa  ;;  a;  a;  a;

3  fj  dk  sl  a;  fjdksla;  jfkdls;a  ;a  ;s  kd  j
4  f  j  fjf  d  k  dkd  s  l  sls  a  ;  fj  dk  sl  a;a

5  a;  al  ak  aj  s  s;  sl  sk  sj  d  d;  dl  dk  djd
6  ja  js  jd  jf  k  ka  ks  kd  kf  l  la  ls  ld  lfl

7  f  fa  fad  s  sa  sad  f  fa  fall  fall  l  la  lad  s  sa  sad
8  a  as  ask  a  ad  add  j  ja  jak  f  fa  fall;  ask;  add  jak
```

▤ Skillbuilding

1Rb Keyboard Review

Key each line once; repeat as time permits.

```
9   ik  ki  ki  ik  is  if  id  il  ij  ia  ij  ik  is  if  ji  id  ia
10  is  il  ill  sill  dill  fill  sid  lid  ail  lid  slid  jail

11  if  is  il  kid  kids  ill  kid  if  kids;  if  a  kid  is  ill
12  is  id  if  ai  aid  jaks  lid  sid  sis  did  ail;  if  lids;

13  a  lass;  ask  dad;  lads  ask  dad;  a  fall;  fall  salads
14  as  a  fad;  ask  a  lad;  a  lass;  all  add;  a  kid;  skids

15  as  asks  did  disk  ail  fail  sail  ails  jail  sill  silk
16  ask  dad;  dads  said;  is  disk;  kiss  a  lad;  salad  lid

17  aid  a  lad;  if  a  kid  is;  a  salad  lid;  kiss  sad  dads
18  as  ad  all  ask  jak  lad  fad  kids  ill  kill  fall  disks
```

COMMUNICATION SKILLS 1

 **Capitalization Guides**

Capitalize:

1. **First word of a sentence and of a direct quotation.**

   We were tolerating instead of managing diversity.

   The speaker said, "We must value diversity, not merely recognize it."

2. **Proper nouns**—specific persons, places, or things.

   Common nouns: continent, river, car, street

   Proper nouns: Asia, Mississippi, Buick, State St.

   Exception: Capitalize a title of high distinction even when it does not refer to a specific person (e.g., President of the United States).

3. **Derivatives** of proper nouns and capitalize **geographical** names.

   Derivatives: American history, German food, English accent, Ohio Valley

   Proper nouns: Tampa, Florida, Mount Rushmore

4. **A personal or professional title** when it precedes the name; capitalize a title of high distinction without a name.

   Title: Lieutenant Kahn, Mayor Walsh, Doctor Welby

   High distinction: the President of the United States,

5. **Days of the week, months of the year, holidays, periods of history, and historic events.**

   Monday, June 8, Labor Day, Renaissance

6. **Specific parts of the country** but not compass points that show direction.

   Midwest   the South   northwest of town   the Middle East

7. **Family relationships** when used with a person's name.

   Aunt Carol   my mother   Uncle Mark

8. **A noun preceding a figure** except for common nouns such as line, page, and sentence.

   Unit 1   Section 2   page 2   verse 7   line 2

9. **First and main words of side headings, titles of books, and works of art.** Do not capitalize words of four or fewer letters that are conjunctions, prepositions, or articles.

   Computers in the News   *Raiders of the Lost Ark*

10. **Names of organizations and specific departments** within the writer's organization.

    Girl Scouts   our Sales Department

11. **The salutation of a letter and the first word of the complimentary closing.**

    Dear Mr. Bush   Ladies and Gentlemen: Sincerely yours,

    Very cordially yours,

Lesson 2 | E and N

W a r m u p

2a

1. Open *Keyboarding Pro*.
2. Locate your student record.
3. Select Lesson 2.

1 ff dd ss aa ff dd ss aa jj kk ll ;; fj dk sl a; a;

2 fj dk sl a; fjdksla; a;sldkfj fj dk sl a; fjdksla;

3 aa ss dd ff jj kk ll ;; aa ss dd ff jj kk ll ;; a;

4 if a; as is; kids did; ask a sad lad; if a lass is

New Keys

2b E and N

Key each line once; DS between groups.

e Reach *up* with *left second* finger.

e

5 e ed ed led led lea lea ale ale elf elf eke eke ed

6 e el el eel els elk elk lea leak ale kale led jell

7 e ale kale lea leak fee feel lea lead elf self eke

n

8 n nj nj an an and and fan fan and kin din fin land

9 n an fan in fin and land sand din fans sank an sin

10 n in ink sink inn kin skin an and land in din dink

n Reach down with right first finger.

all reaches learned

11 den end fen ken dean dens ales fend fens keen knee

12 if in need; feel ill; as an end; a lad and a lass;

13 and sand; a keen idea; as a sail sank; is in jail;

14 an idea; an end; a lake; a nail; a jade; a dean is

2c Textbook Keying

Key each line once; DS between groups. Repeat.

15 if a lad;
16 is a sad fall

17 if a lass did ask
18 ask a lass; ask a lad

19 a;sldkfj a;sldkfj a;sldkfj
20 a; sl dk fj fj dk sl a; a;sldkfj

21 i ik ik if if is is kid skid did lid aid laid said
22 ik kid ail die fie did lie ill ilk silk skill skid

> Reach with little finger; tap Enter key quickly; return finger to home key.

Key the report, following the Report Format Guides. Save as **Drill 11**.

about 2.1" top margin

ELECTRONIC MAIL GUIDELINES ⟵ 14pt

Electronic mail, a widely used communication channel, clearly has three major advantages—time effectiveness, distance effectiveness, and cost-effectiveness. To reap full benefit from this popular and convenient communication medium, follow the basic guidelines regarding the creation and use of e-mail.

DS

Side heading

E-mail Composition

DS

Default or 1"

Although perceived as informal documents, e-mail messages are business records. Therefore, follow effective communication guidelines: write clear, concise sentences; break the message into logical paragraphs; and double-space between paragraphs. Spell check e-mail messages carefully, and verify punctuation and content accuracy. Do limit e-mail messages to one idea per message, and preferably limit to one screen. Include a subject line that clearly defines the e-mail message.

Default or 1"

DS

Side heading

E-mail Practices

DS

Although many people are using e-mail, some individuals do not use it as their preferred method of communication and may check it infrequently. To accomplish tasks more effectively, be aware of individuals' preferred channels of communication and use those channels. Consider an e-mail message the property of the sender, and forward only with permission. Some senders include a note in the signature line that reminds recipients not to forward e-mail without seeking permission.

2d Open Screen

The **Open Screen** is a word processor. Exercises to be keyed in the Open Screen are identified with an Open Screen icon. For these exercises, follow the instructions in the textbook and key from your textbook. Keep your eyes on the textbook copy as you key—not on your fingers or the screen.

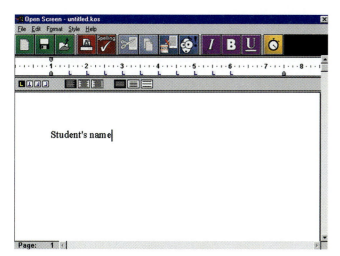

1. Click the **Open Screen** button at the left edge of the Main Menu of *Keyboarding Pro*.
2. Key your name and strike ENTER twice.
3. Follow the directions in the textbook for the drill.
4. Print what you key in the Open Screen.
5. Click the **Close** button in the upper-right corner to exit the Open Screen.

Skillbuilding

2e Reinforcement

1. In the Open Screen, key each line twice. DS between groups of two lines.
2. Print but do not save the exercise.
3. Close the Open Screen and you will return to Lesson 2 in the software.

TECHNIQUE TIP

Keep your eyes on the textbook copy.

i

23 ik ik ik if is il ik id is if kid did lid aid ails

24 did lid aid; add a line; aid kids; ill kids; id is

n

25 nj nj nj an an and and end den ken in ink sin skin

26 jn din sand land nail sank and dank skin sans sink

e

27 el els elf elk lea lead fee feel sea seal ell jell

28 el eke ale jak lake elf els jaks kale eke els lake

all reaches

29 dine in an inn; fake jade; lend fans; as sand sank

30 in nine inns; if an end; need an idea; seek a fee;

2f End the lesson

1. Print the Lesson Report.
2. Exit the software; remove the storage disk if appropriate.

Document Design

Report Format Guides

Unbound Report Format

Reports prepared without binders are called **unbound reports**. Unbound reports may be attached with a staple or paper clip in the upper-left corner.

Margins, Spacing, and Page Numbers

Top margins: Approximately 2" for the first page; strike ENTER to position the insertion point; 1" for second and succeeding pages.

Side margins: Default margins 1.25" or 1".

Bottom margins: Approximately 1"; last page bottom margin may be deeper.

Font size and spacing: Use 12-point size for readability. Generally, educational reports are double spaced (DS) and business reports are single spaced (SS). Indent paragraphs 0.5" when the body of the report is DS. Begin the paragraphs at the left margin when the report is SS, and DS between paragraphs.

Enumerated items: Align bulleted or numbered items with the beginning of a paragraph. SS each item and DS between items.

Page numbers: The first page of a report is not numbered. The second and succeeding pages are numbered in the upper-right corner in the header position.

Main heading

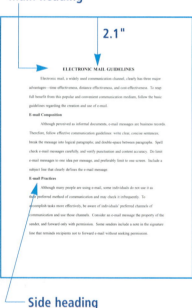

2.1"

Side heading

Headings

Headings have a hierarchy. Spacing and font size indicate the level of heading. The main heading informs readers of the report title. Side headings within the report break a lengthy report into smaller, easier-to-understand parts.

Main heading: Center and key the title in ALL CAPS. Use 14 point and bold.

Side headings: Key at left margin in bold. Capitalize the first letters of main words; DS above and below side headings if the report is SS.

Title Page

The cover or title page should have a concise title that identifies the report to the reader. A title page includes the title of the report, the name and title of the individual or the organization for which the report was prepared, the name and title of the writer, and the date the report was completed.

Center-align each line and center the page vertically. Allow near equal space between parts of the page (strike ENTER about eight times).

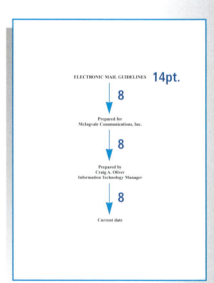

LESSON 3 | Review

✳ Warmup

3a

Key each line at a steady pace; strike and release each key quickly. Key each line again at a faster pace.

home 1 ad ads lad fad dad as ask fa la lass jak jaks alas

n 2 an fan and land fan flan sans sand sank flank dank

i 3 is id ill dill if aid ail fail did kid ski lid ilk

all 4 ade alas nine else fife ken; jell ink jak inns if;

▤ Skillbuilding

3b Rhythm Builder

Key each line twice.

Lines 5–8: Think and key words. Make the space part of the word.

Lines 9–12: Think and key phrases. Do not key the vertical rules separating the phrases.

easy words

5 if is as an ad el and did die eel fin fan elf lens

6 as ask and id kid and ade aid eel feel ilk skis an

7 ail fail aid did ken ale led an flan inn inns alas

8 eel eke nee kneel did kids kale sees lake elf fled

easy phrases

9 el el|id id|is is|eke eke|lee lee|ale ale|jill jill

10 is if|is a|is a|a disk|a disk|did ski|did ski|is a

11 sell a|sell a|sell a sled|fall fad|fall fad|did die

12 sees a lake|sees a lake|as a deal|sell a sled|all a

3c Technique Practice

Key each 2-line group twice; SS.

> **TECHNIQUE TIP**
>
> Reach with the little finger; tap [Enter] key quickly; return finger to home key.

home row: fingers curved and upright

13 jak lad as lass dad sad lads fad fall la ask ad as

14 asks add jaks dads a lass ads flak adds sad as lad

upward reaches: straighten fingers slightly; return quickly to home position

15 fed die led ail kea lei did ale fife silk leak lie

16 sea lid deal sine desk lie ale like life idea jail

double letters: don't hurry when stroking double letters

17 fee jell less add inn seek fall alee lass keel all

18 dill dell see fell eel less all add kiss seen sell

Key the letter at right following the Business Letter Guides. Save as **Drill 10**.

2.1" or center vertically

E-Market, Group
10 East Rivercenter Boulevard
Covington, KY 41016-8765

Dateline — Current date ↓4

Letter address — Mr. Ishmal Dabdoub
Professional Office Consultants
1782 Laurel Canyon Road
Sunnyvale, CA 93785-9087 **DS**

Salutation — Dear Mr. Dabdoub **DS**

Body — Have you heard your friends and colleagues talk about obtaining real-time stock quotes? real-time account balances and positions? Nasdaq Level II quotes? extended-hours trading? If so, then they are among the three million serious investors that have opened an account with E-Market. **DS**

We believe that the best decisions are informed decisions made in a timely manner. E-Market has an online help desk that provides information for all levels of investors, from beginners to the experienced serious trader. You can learn basic tactics for investing in the stock market, how to avoid common mistakes, and pick up some advanced strategies. **DS**

Stay on top of the market and your investments! Visit our web site at http://www.emarket.com to learn more about our banking and brokerage services. E-Market Group is the premier site for online investing. **DS**

Complementary Closing — Sincerely ↓4

Margaritta Gibson

Writer's name — Ms. Margaritta Gibson
Title — Marketing Manager **DS**

Reference initials — xx

Repetitive stress injury (RSI)

Repetitive stress injury (RSI) is a result of repeated movement of a particular part of the body. A familiar example is "tennis elbow." Of more concern to keyboard users is the form of RSI called **carpal tunnel syndrome (CTS)**.

CTS is an inflammatory disease that develops gradually and affects the wrist, hands, and forearms. Blood vessels, tendons, and nerves pass into the hand through the carpal tunnel (see illustration below). If any of these structures enlarge or if the walls of the tunnel narrow, the median nerve is pinched, and CTS symptoms may result.

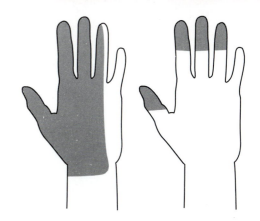

Areas affected by carpal tunnel syndrome

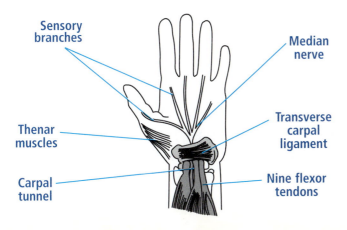

Sensory branches

Median nerve

Thenar muscles

Transverse carpal ligament

Carpal tunnel

Nine flexor tendons

Palm view of left hand

Causes of RSI/CTS

RSI/CTS often develops in workers whose physical routine is unvaried. Common occupational factors include: (1) using awkward posture, (2) using poor techniques, (3) performing tasks with wrists bent (*see below*), (4) using improper equipment, (5) working at a rapid pace, (6) not taking rest breaks, and (7) not doing exercises that promote graceful motion and good techniques.

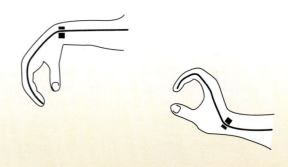

Improper wrist positions for keystroking

Symptoms of RSI/CTS

CTS symptoms include numbness in the hand; tingling or burning in the hand, wrist, or elbow; severe pain in the forearm, elbow, or shoulder; and difficulty in gripping objects. Symptoms usually appear during sleeping hours, probably because many people sleep with their wrists flexed.

If not properly treated, the pressure on the median nerve, which controls the thumb, forefinger, middle finger, and half the ring finger (see top right), causes severe pain. The pain can radiate into the forearm, elbow, or shoulder and can require surgery or result in permanent damage or paralysis.

Other factors associated with CTS include a person's genetic makeup; the aging process; hormonal influences; obesity; chronic diseases such as rheumatoid arthritis and gout; misaligned fractures; and hobbies such as gardening, knitting, and woodworking that require the same motion over and over. CTS affects over three times more women than men, with 60 percent of the affected persons between the ages of 30 and 60.

APPENDIX

LESSON 19 | $ and - (hyphen), Number Expression

Warmup

19a

Key each line twice SS.

alphabet 1 Why did the judge quiz poor Victor about his blank tax form?

figures 2 J. Boyd, Ph.D., changed Items 10, 57, 36, and 48 on page 92.

3d row 3 To try the tea, we hope to tour the port prior to the party.

easy 4 Did he signal the authentic robot to do a turn to the right?

| 1 | 2 | 3 | 4 | 5 | 6 | 7 | 8 | 9 | 10 | 11 | 12 |

New Keys

19b $ and -

Key each line once SS;
DS between 2-line groups.

> - = hyphen
> -- = dash
> Do not space before or after a hyphen or a dash.

$ Shift; then reach up with *left first* finger.

- (hyphen) Reach up with *right fourth* finger.

$

5 $ $f f$ $ $; if $4; half $4; off $4; of $4; $4 fur; $4 flats

6 for $8; cost $9; log $3; grab $10; give Rolf $2; give Viv $4

7 Since she paid $45 for the item priced at $54, she saved $9.

- (hyphen)

8 - -; ;- - - -; up-to-date; co-op; father-in-law; four-square

9 pop-up foul; big-time job; snap-on bit; one- or two-hour ski

10 You need 6 signatures--half of the members--on the petition.

all symbols learned

11 I paid $10 for the low-cost disk; high-priced ones cost $40.

12 Le-An spent $20 for travel, $95 for books, and $38 for food.

13 Mr. Loft-Smit sold his boat for $467; he bought it for $176.

Skillbuilding

19c Keyboard Reinforcement

Key each line once; repeat the drill.

e/d 14 Edie discreetly decided to deduct expenses in making a deed.

w/e 15 Working women wear warm wool sweaters when weather dictates.

r/e 16 We heard very rude remarks regarding her recent termination.

s/d 17 This seal's sudden misdeeds destroyed several goods on land.

v/b 18 Beverley voted by giving a bold beverage to every brave boy.

18d Rhythm Builder
Key each line twice SS; DS between 2-line groups; repeat.

word response: *think* and *key* words

19 he el id is go us it an me of he of to if ah or bye do so am
20 Did she enamel emblems on a big panel for the downtown sign?

stroke response: *think* and *key* each stroke

21 kin are hip read lymph was pop saw ink art oil gas up as mop
22 Barbara started the union wage earners tax in Texas in July.

combination response: vary speed but maintain rhythm

23 upon than eve lion when burley with they only them loin were
24 It was the opinion of my neighbor that we may work as usual.

18e Diagnostic Writing

Return to the Numeric Lesson menu. Click the **Diagnostic Writings** button. Key the paragraph as a 3' Diagnostic Writing.
Goals: 1', 17–23 *gwam*
2', 15–21 *gwam*
3', 14–20 *gwam*

all letters

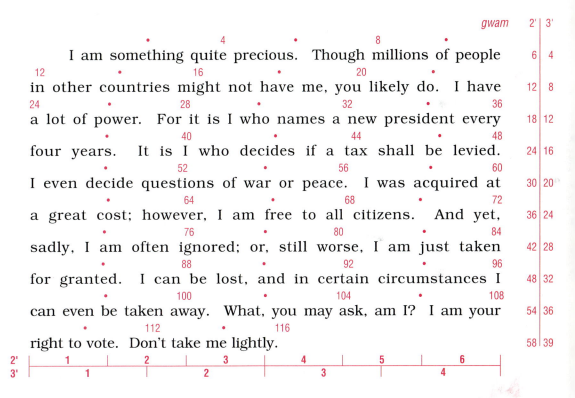

	gwam	2'	3'
I am something quite precious. Though millions of people		6	4
in other countries might not have me, you likely do. I have		12	8
a lot of power. For it is I who names a new president every		18	12
four years. It is I who decides if a tax shall be levied.		24	16
I even decide questions of war or peace. I was acquired at		30	20
a great cost; however, I am free to all citizens. And yet,		36	24
sadly, I am often ignored; or, still worse, I am just taken		42	28
for granted. I can be lost, and in certain circumstances I		48	32
can even be taken away. What, you may ask, am I? I am your		54	36
right to vote. Don't take me lightly.		58	39

Communication

18f Composition

1. Go to the Open Screen.
2. Introduce yourself to your instructor by composing two paragraphs, each containing about three sentences. Use proper grammatical structure. Do not worry about keying errors at this time.
3. Save the document as **xx-profile**. It is not necessary to print the document. You will open and print it in a later lesson.

19d Speed Builder

Key each line once, working for fluid, consistent stroking. Repeat at a faster speed.

easy words

19 am it go bus dye jam irk six sod tic yam ugh spa vow aid dug
20 he or by air big elf dog end fit and lay sue toe wit own got
21 six foe pen firm also body auto form down city kept make fog.

easy phrases

22 it is|if the|and also|to me|the end|to us|if it|it is|to the
23 if it is|to the end|do you wish|to go to|for the end|to make
24 lay down|he or she|make me|by air|end of|by me|kept it|of me

easy sentences

25 Did the chap work to mend the torn right half of the ensign?
26 Blame me for their penchant for the antique chair and panel.
27 She bid by proxy for eighty bushels of a corn and rye blend.

Communication

Spell out numbers:

19e Number Expression

1. Study the rules and examples at the right.
2. In the Open Screen, key the information below at the left margin. Press ENTER as shown.

   Your name ENTER

   Current date ENTER

   Skillbuilders 1, Drill 6

   ENTER ENTER

3. Key the sample sentences 28–33. Backspace to correct errors.
4. Change figures to words as needed in sentences 34–36.
5. Save the file as **xx-19e**.

1. **First word in a sentence.** Key numbers ten and lower as words unless they are part of a series of related numbers, any of which are over ten.

   Three of the four members were present.

   She wrote 12 stories and 2 plays in five years.

2. The **smaller of two adjacent numbers** as words.

   SolVir shipped six 24-ton engines.

3. **Isolated fractions and approximate numbers.** Key as words **large round numbers that can be expressed as one or two words.** Hyphenate fractions expressed as words.

   She completed one-fourth of the experiments.

   Val sent out three hundred invitations.

4. **Preceding "o'clock".**

   John's due at four o'clock. Pick him up at 4:15 p.m.

28 **Six** or **seven** older players were cut from the **37**-member team.
29 I have **2** of **14** coins I need to start my set. Kristen has **9.**
30 Of **nine 24**-ton engines ordered, we shipped **six** last Tuesday.
31 Shelly has read just **one-half** of about **forty-five** documents.
32 The **six** boys sent well over **two hundred** printed invitations.
33 **One** or **two** of us will be on duty from **two** until **six** o'clock.
34 The meeting begins promptly at 9. We plan 4 sessions.
35 The 3-person crew cleaned 6 stands, 12 tables, and 13 desks.
36 The 3d meeting is at 3 o'clock on Friday, February 2.

LESSON 18 | 3 and 6

☀ Warmup

18a
Key each line twice SS.

alphabet 1 Jim Kable won a second prize for his very quixotic drawings.

figures 2 If 57 of the 105 boys go on July 29, 48 of them will remain.

easy 3 With the usual bid, I paid for a quantity of big world maps.

| 1 | 2 | 3 | 4 | 5 | 6 | 7 | 8 | 9 | 10 | 11 | 12 |

▣ New Keys

18b 3 and 6
Key each line once SS.

3 Reach *up* with *left second* finger.

6 Reach *up* with *right first* finger.

3

4 3 3d d3 3 3; had 3 days; did 3 dives; led 3 dogs; add 3 dips

5 we 3 ride 3 cars; take 33 dials; read 3 copies; save 33 days

6 On July 3, 33 lights lit 33 stands holding 33 prize winners.

6

7 6 6j 6j 6 6; 6 jays; 6 jams; 6 jigs; 6 jibs; 6 jots; 6 jokes

8 only 6 high; on 66 units; reach 66 numbers; 6 yams or 6 jams

9 On May 6, Car 66 delivered 66 tons of No. 6 shale to Pier 6.

all figures learned

10 At 6 p.m., Channel 3 reported the August 6 score was 6 to 3.

11 Jean, do Items 28 and 6; Mika, 59 and 10; Kyle, 3, 4, and 7.

12 Cars 56 and 34 used Aisle 9; Cars 2 and 87 can use Aisle 10.

▣ Skillbuilding

18c Keyboard Reinforcement
Key each line once; DS between groups of three.

> **TECHNIQUE TIP**
> Make the long reaches without returning to the home row between reaches.

long reaches

13 ce cede cedar wreck nu nu nut punt nuisance my my amy mystic

14 ny ny any many company mu mu mull lumber mulch br br furbish

15 The absence of receiving my umbrella disturbed the musician.

number review

16 set 0; push 4; Car 00; score 44; jot 04; age 40; Billet 4004

17 April 5; lock 5; set 66; fill 55; hit 65; pick 56; adds 5665

18 Her grades are 93, 87, and 100; his included 82, 96, and 54.

LESSON 20 | # and /

✳ W a r m u p

20a
Key each line twice SS
(slowly, then faster).

alphabet 1 Freda Jencks will have money to buy six quite large topazes.

symbols 2 I bought 10 ribbons and 45 disks from Cable-Han Co. for $78.

home row 3 Dallas sold jade flasks; Sal has a glass flask full of salt.

easy 4 He may cycle down to the field by the giant oak and cut hay.

▣ New Keys

20b # and /
Key each line once SS.

= number sign, pounds

/ = diagonal, slash

\# Shift; then reach *up* with *left second* finger.

/ Reach *down* with *right fourth* finger.

#

5 # #e e# # # #; had #3 dial; did #3 drop; set #3 down; Bid #3

6 leave #82; sold #20; Lyric #16; bale #34; load #53; Optic #7

7 Notice #333 says to load Car #33 with 33# of #3 grade shale.

/

8 / /; ;/ / / /; 1/2; 1/3; Mr./Mrs.; 1/5/94; 22 11/12; and/or;

9 to/from; /s/ William Smit; 2/10, n/30; his/her towels; 6 1/2

10 The numerals 1 5/8, 3 1/4, and 60 7/9 are "mixed fractions."

all symbols learned

11 Invoice #737 cites 15 2/3# of rye was shipped C.O.D. 4/6/95.

12 B-O-A Company's Check #50/5 for $87 paid for 15# of #3 wire.

13 Our Co-op List #20 states $40 for 16 1/2 crates of tomatoes.

▣ Skillbuilding

20c Keyboard Reinforcement

Key each line once; work for fluency.

Option: In the Open Screen, key 30" writings on both lines of a pair. Work to avoid pauses.

gwam 30"

14 She did the key work at the height of the problem. 20

15 Form #726 is the title to the island; she owns it. 20

16 The rock is a form of fuel; he did enrich it with coal. 22

17 The corn-and-turkey dish is a blend of turkey and corn. 22

18 It is right to work to end the social problems of the world. 24

19 If I sign it on 3/19, the form can aid us to pay the 40 men. 24

17d Technique Reinforcement

Key smoothly; strike the keys at a brisk, steady pace.

first finger

19 buy them gray vent guy brunt buy brunch much give huge vying
20 Hagen, after her July triumph at tennis, may try volleyball.
21 Verna urges us to buy yet another of her beautiful rag rugs.

second finger

22 keen idea; kick it back; ice breaker; decide the issue; cite
23 Did Dick ask Cecelia, his sister, if she decided to like me?
24 Suddenly, Micki's bike skidded on the Cedar Street ice rink.

third/fourth finger

25 low slow lax solo wax zip zap quips quiz zipper prior icicle
26 Paula has always allowed us to relax at La Paz and at Quito.
27 Please ask Zale to explain who explores most aquatic slopes.

17e Speed Builder

1. Key each paragraph in the Open Screen for a 1' writing.
2. Set the Timer for 2'. Take two 2' writings on all paragraphs. Reach for a speed within two words of 1' *gwam*.
3. Take a 3' writing on all paragraphs. Reach for a speed within four words of 1' *gwam*. Print.

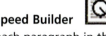

all letters

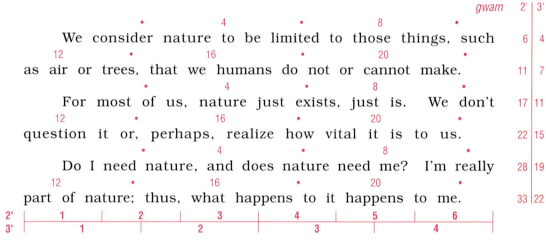

	gwam	2'	3'
We consider nature to be limited to those things, such		6	4
as air or trees, that we humans do not or cannot make.		11	7
For most of us, nature just exists, just is. We don't		17	11
question it or, perhaps, realize how vital it is to us.		22	15
Do I need nature, and does nature need me? I'm really		28	19
part of nature; thus, what happens to it happens to me.		33	22

2' | 1 | 2 | 3 | 4 | 5 | 6 |
3' | 1 | 2 | 3 | 4 |

17f Speed Builder

TECHNIQUE TIP

Keep hands quiet and fingers well curved over the keys. Do not allow your fingers to bounce.

1. In the Open screen, key the information below at the left margin.

Your name   **ENTER**
Current date   **ENTER**
Skillbuilders 1, Drill 2   **ENTER ENTER**

2. Key Drill 2, page 32 from your textbook. Concentrate as you practice on your own, working for good control.

Communication

20d Number Usage Review

DS; decide whether the circled numbers should be keyed as figures or as words and make needed changes. Check your finished work with 19e, page 47.

```
20 Six or (7) older players were cut from the (37)-member team.
21 I have (2) of 14 coins I need to start my set.  Kristen has (9).
22 Of (9) 24-ton engines ordered, we shipped (6) last Tuesday.
23 Shelly has read just (1) half of about (45) documents.
24 The (6) boys sent well over (200) printed invitations.
25 (1) or (2) of us will be on duty from (2) until (6) o'clock.
```

Skillbuilding

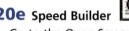

20e Speed Builder

1. Go to the Open Screen.
2. Follow the procedures at the right for increasing your speed by taking guided writings.
3. Take a 3' writing without the guide on the complete writing.

STANDARD PLAN for Guided Writing Procedures

1. In the Open Screen, take a 1' writing on paragraph 1. Note your *gwam*.
2. Add four words to your 1' *gwam* to determine your goal rate.
3. Set the Timer for 1'. Set the Timer option to beep every 15".
4. From the table below, select from Column 4 the speed nearest your goal rate. Note the ¼' point at the left of that speed. Place a light check mark within the paragraphs at the ¼' points.
5. Take two 1' guided writings on paragraphs 1 and 2. Do not save.
6. Turn the beeper off.

			gwam
1/4'	1/2'	3/4'	1'
4	8	12	16
5	10	15	20
6	12	18	24
7	14	21	28
8	16	24	32
9	18	27	36
10	20	30	40

all letters

	gwam 2'	3'	
Some of us think that the best way to get attention is	6	4	35
to try a new style, or to look quixotic, or to be different	12	8	39
somehow. Perhaps we are looking for nothing much more than	18	12	43
acceptance from others of ourselves just the way we now are.	24	16	47
There is no question about it; we all want to look our	29	19	50
best to impress other people. How we achieve this may mean	35	23	54
trying some of this and that; but our basic objective is to	41	27	58
take our raw materials, you and me, and build up from there.	47	31	62

2' | 1 | 2 | 3 | 4 | 5 | 6
3' | 1 | 2 | 3 | 4

LESSON 17 | 4 and 9

Warmup

17a
Key each line twice.

alphabet	1	Bob realized very quickly that jumping was excellent for us.
figures	2	Has each of the 18 clerks now corrected Item 501 on page 27?
shift keys	3	L. K. Coe, M.D., hopes Dr. Lopez can leave for Maine in May.
easy	4	The men paid their own firms for the eight big enamel signs.

New Keys

17b [4] and [9]
Key each line once SS.

4 Reach *up* with *left first* finger.

9 Reach *up* with *right third* finger.

4

5 4 4f f4 4 4 4; if 4 furs; off 4 floors; gaff 4 fish; 4 flags

6 44th floor; half of 44; 4 walked 44 flights; 4 girls; 4 boys

7 I order exactly 44 bagels, 4 cakes, and 4 pies before 4 a.m.

9

8 9 9l l9 9 9 9; fill 9 lugs; call 9 lads; Bill 9 lost; dial 9

9 also 9 oaks; roll 9 loaves; 9.9 degrees; sell 9 oaks; Hall 9

10 Just 9 couples, 9 men and 9 women, left at 9 on our Tour 99.

all figures learned

11 Memo 94 says 9 pads, 4 pens, and 4 ribbons were sent July 9.

12 Study Item 17 and Item 28 on page 40 and Item 59 on page 49.

13 Within 17 months he drove 85 miles, walked 29, and flew 490.

Skillbuilding

17c Figure Keyreaches
Key each line twice; DS between 2-line groups.

14 My staff of *18* worked *11* hours a day from May *27* to June *12*.

15 There were *5* items tested by Inspector *7* at *4* p.m. on May *8*.

16 Please send her File *10* today at *8*; her access number is *97*.

17 Car *47* had its trial run. The qualifying speed was *198* mph.

18 The estimated score? *485*. Actual? *190*. Difference? *295*.

LESSON 21 | % and !

Warmup
21a
Key each line twice SS.

alphabet	1	Merry will have picked out a dozen quarts of jam for boxing.
fig/sym	2	Jane-Ann bought 16 7/8 yards of #240 cotton at $3.59 a yard.
1st row	3	Can't brave, zany Cave Club men/women next climb Mt. Zamban?
easy	4	Did she rush to cut six bushels of corn for the civic corps?

New Keys

21b % and !
Key each line once SS.

% Shift; then reach up with *left first* finger.

> **% = percent sign:** Use % with business forms or where space is restricted; otherwise, use the word "percent." Space twice after the exclamation point!

%

5 % %f f% % %; off 5%; if 5%; of 5% fund; half 5%; taxes of 5%

6 7% rent; 3% tariff; 9% F.O.B.; 15% greater; 28% base; up 46%

7 Give discounts of 5% on rods, 50% on lures, and 75% on line.

! reach *up* with the *left fourth* finger

8 ! !a a! ! ! !; Eureka! Ha! No! Pull 10! Extra! America!

9 Listen to the call! Now! Ready! Get set! Go! Good show!

10 I want it now, not next week! I am sure to lose 50% or $19.

all symbols

11 The ad offers a 10% discount, but this notice says 15% less!

12 He got the job! With Clark's Supermarket! Please call Mom!

13 Bill #92-44 arrived very late from Zyclone; it was paid 7/4.

21c Keyboard Reinforcement
Key each line once; work for fluency.

> **SPACING TIP**
> - Do not space between a figure and the % or $ signs.
> - Do not space before or after the dash.

all symbols

14 As of 6/28, Jeri owes $31 for dinner and $27 for cab fare.

15 Invoice #20--it was dated 3/4--billed $17 less 15% discount.

16 He deducted 2% instead of 6%, a clear saving of 6% vs. 7%.

combination response

17 Look at my dismal grade in English; but I guess I earned it.

18 Kris started to blend a cocoa beverage for a shaken cowhand.

19 Jan may make a big profit if she owns the title to the land.

Skillbuilding

16d Reach Review
Key each line once; fingers curved and relaxed; wrists low.

16e Rhythm Builder
Key each line twice; do not pause at the end of lines.

TECHNIQUE TIP
Think and key the words and phrases as units rather than letter by letter.

3d/4th
19 pop was lap pass slaw wool solo swap apollo wasp load plaque
20 Al's quote was, "I was dazzled by the jazz, pizza, and pool."

1st/2d
21 bad fun nut kick dried night brick civic thick hutch believe
22 Kim may visit her friends in Germany if I give her a ticket.

3d/1st
23 cry tube wine quit very curb exit crime ebony mention excite
24 To be invited, petition the six executive committee members.

words: *think, say,* and *key* words

25 is do am lay cut pen dub may fob ale rap cot hay pay hem box
26 box wit man sir fish also hair giant rigor civic virus ivory
27 laugh sight flame audit formal social turkey bicycle problem

phrases: *think, say,* and *key* phrases

28 is it|is it|if it is|if it is|or by|or by|or me|or me|for us
29 and all|for pay|pay dues and|the pen|the pen box|the pen box
30 such forms|held both|work form|then wish|sign name|with them

easy sentences

31 The man is to do the work right; he then pays the neighbors.
32 Sign the forms to pay the eight men for the turkey and hams.
33 The antique ivory bicycle is a social problem for the chair.

| 1 | 2 | 3 | 4 | 5 | 6 | 7 | 8 | 9 | 10 | 11 | 12 |

16f Speed Check
1. Take two 1' writings on paragraph 1.
2. Take two 1' writings on paragraph 2.
3. Take one 2' writing on both paragraphs.

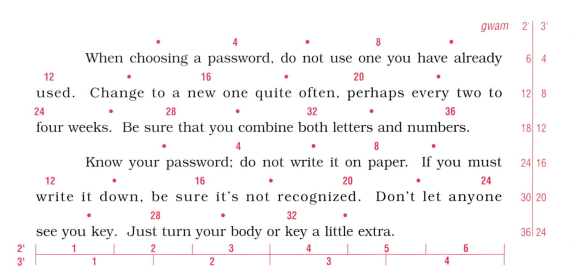

gwam 2' 3'

When choosing a password, do not use one you have already   6   4
used. Change to a new one quite often, perhaps every two to   12   8
four weeks. Be sure that you combine both letters and numbers. 18 12

Know your password; do not write it on paper. If you must   24 16
write it down, be sure it's not recognized. Don't let anyone 30 20
see you key. Just turn your body or key a little extra.   36 24

Skillbuilding

21d **Reach Mastery**

Key each set of lines SS; DS between each group; fingers curved, hands quiet. Repeat if time permits.

1st finger

20 by bar get fun van for inn art from gray hymn July true verb
21 brag human bring unfold hominy mighty report verify puny joy
22 You are brave to try bringing home the van in the bad storm.

2d finger

23 ace ink did cad keyed deep seed kind Dick died kink like kid
24 cease decease decades kick secret check decide kidney evaded
25 Dedre likes the idea of ending dinner with cake for dessert.

3d finger

26 oil sow six vex wax axe low old lox pool west loss wool slow
27 swallow swamp saw sew wood sax sexes loom stew excess school
28 Wes waxes floors and washes windows at low costs to schools.

4th finger

29 zap zip craze pop pup pan daze quote queen quiz pizza puzzle
30 zoo graze zipper panzer zebra quip partizan patronize appear
31 Czar Zane appears to be dazzled by the apple pizza and jazz.

21e **Speed Runs with Numbers**

Take 1' writings; the last number you key when you stop is your approximate *gwam*.

1 and 2 and 3 and 4 and 5 and 6 and 7 and 8 and 9 and 10 and
11 and 12 and 13 and 14 and 15 and 16 and 17 and 18 and 19
and 20 and 21 and 22 and 23 and 24 and 25 and 26 and 27 and

21f **Speed Check**

Key a 1' and 3' writing.

all letters

	gwam	1'	2'
Teams are the basic unit of performance for a firm.	11	5	42
They are not the solution to all of the organizational needs.	23	12	48
They will not solve all of the problems, but it is known	35	17	54
that a team can perform at a higher rate than other groups.	47	23	60
It is one of the best ways to support the changes needed for	59	30	66
a firm. The team must have time in order to make	71	36	72
a quality working plan.	74	37	74

```
1' |  1  |  2  |  3  |  4  |  5  |  6  |  7  |  8  |  9  | 10  | 11  | 12
2' |     1     |     2     |     3     |     4     |     5     |     6
```

LESSON 16 | 2 and 7

 W a r m u p

16a
Key each line twice SS.

alphabet 1	Perry might know I feel jinxed because I have missed a quiz.
figures 2	Channels 5 and 8, on from 10 to 11, said Luisa's IQ was 150.
caps lock 3	Ella Hill will see Chekhov's THE CHERRY ORCHARD on Czech TV.
easy 4	The big dog by the bush kept the ducks and hen in the field.

| 1 | 2 | 3 | 4 | 5 | 6 | 7 | 8 | 9 | 10 | 11 | 12 |

New Keys

16b 2 and 7
Key each line once SS.

2 Reach *up* with *left third* finger.

7 Reach *down* with *right first* finger.

2

5 2 2s s2 2 2; has 2 sons; is 2 sizes; was 2 sites; has 2 skis
6 add 2 and 2; 2 sets of 2; catch 22; as 2 of the 22; 222 Main
7 Exactly at 2 on August 22, the 22d Company left from Pier 2.

7

8 7 7j j7 7 7; 7 jets; 7 jeans; 7 jays; 7 jobs; 7 jars; 7 jaws
9 ask for 7; buy 7; 77 years; June 7; take any 7; deny 77 boys
10 From May 7 on, all 77 men will live at 777 East 77th Street.

all figures learned

11 I read 2 of the 72 books, Ellis read 7, and Han read all 72.
12 Tract 27 cites the date as 1850; Tract 170 says it was 1852.
13 You can take Flight 850 on January 12; I'll take Flight 705.

16c Number Reinforcement
Key each line twice SS (slowly, then faster); DS between 2-line groups.

8/1 14 line 8; Book 1; No. 88; Seat 11; June 18; Cart 81; date 1881
2/7 15 take 2; July 7; buy 22; sell 77; mark 27; adds 72; Memo 2772
5/0 16 feed 5; bats 0; age 50; Ext. 55; File 50; 55 bags; band 5005
all 17 I work 18 visual signs with 20 turns of the 57 lenses to 70.
all 18 Did 17 boys fix the gears for 50 bicycles in 28 racks or 10?

LESSON 22 | (and) and Backspace Key

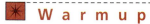

Warmup

22a

Key each line twice SS.

alphabet	1	Avoid lazy punches; expert fighters jab with a quick motion.
fig/sym	2	Be-Low's Bill #483/7 was $96.90, not $102--they took 5% off.
caps lock	3	Report titles may be shown in ALL CAPS; as, BOLD WORD POWER.
easy	4	Do they blame me for their dismal social and civic problems?
		| 1 | 2 | 3 | 4 | 5 | 6 | 7 | 8 | 9 | 10 | 11 | 12 |

New Keys

22b (and)
(parentheses)

Key each line once SS.

> **( ) = parentheses**
> Parentheses indicate offhand, aside, or explanatory messages.

(Shift; then reach up with the *right third* finger.

) Shift; then reach up with the *right fourth* finger.

5 ((l l((; (; Reach from l for the left parenthesis; as, ((.
6)); ;))); Reach from ; for the right parenthesis; as,)).

( )

7 Learn to use parentheses (plural) or parenthesis (singular).
8 The red (No. 34) and blue (No. 78) cars both won here (Rio).
9 We (Galen and I) dined (bagels) in our penthouse (the dorm).

all symbols learned

10 The jacket was $35 (thirty-five dollars)--the tie was extra.
11 Starting 10/29, you can sell Model #49 at a discount of 25%.
12 My size 8 1/2 shoe--a blue pump--was soiled (but not badly).

22c Number and Symbol Reinforcement

Key each line twice, keeping eyes on copy. DS between pairs.

13 Jana has one hard-to-get copy of her hot-off-the-press book.
14 An invoice said that "We give discounts of 10%, 5%, and 3%."
15 The company paid Bill 3/18 on 5/2/97 and Bill 3/1 on 3/6/97.
16 The catalog lists as out of stock Items #230, #710, and #13.
17 Elyn had $8; Sean, $9; and Cal, $7. The cash total was $24.

Skillbuilding

15d Keyboard Reinforcement

Key each line twice SS (slowly, then faster); DS between 2-line groups.

improve figures

20 Read pages 5 and 8; duplicate page 18; omit pages 50 and 51.
21 We have Model 80 with 10 meters or Model 180 with 15 meters.
22 After May 18, French 050 meets in room 15 at 10 a.m. daily.

improve long reaches

23 Barb Abver saw a vibrant version of her brave venture on TV.
24 Call a woman or a man who will manage Minerva Manor in Nome.
25 We were quick to squirt a quantity of water at Quin and West.

15e Tab Review

1. Read the instructions to clear and set tabs.
2. Set a left tab at 4".
3. Practice the lines; strike TAB without watching your keyboard.

STANDARD PLAN for Setting and Clearing Tabs in the Open Screen

Preset or default tabs are displayed on the Ruler. If necessary, display the Ruler in the Open Screen. (Choose the **Show Ruler** option on the Format menu.) Sometimes you will want to remove or clear existing tabs before setting new ones.

To clear and set tabs:

1. On the menu bar, click **Format**, then **Clear All Tabs**.
2. To set tabs, select the type of tab you want to set (left, center, decimal, or right) shown at the lower-left side of the ruler.
3. Click the Ruler at the location where you want to set a tab.

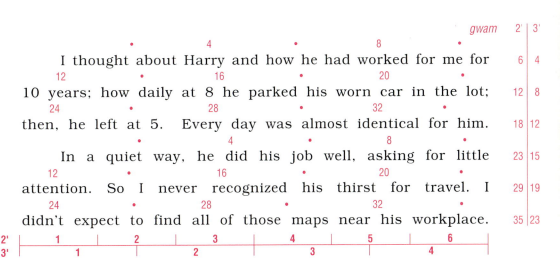

Set tab 4"

                                   → Tab Keyboarding
has become ───────────────→ Tab the primary
means of ─────────────────→ Tab written communication
in business and──────────────→ Tab in our personal lives.
Keyboarding is───────────────→ Tab used by persons
in every profession ────────────→ Tab and most job levels.

15f Speed Check

1. Click the Open Screen button.
2. Take two 1' writings on paragraph 2. Note your *gwam*.
3. Take two 1' writings on paragraph 1. Try to equal paragraph 2 rate.
4. Take one 2' writing on both paragraphs.

  all letters

	gwam	2'	3'
I thought about Harry and how he had worked for me for		6	4
10 years; how daily at 8 he parked his worn car in the lot;		12	8
then, he left at 5. Every day was almost identical for him.		18	12
In a quiet way, he did his job well, asking for little		23	15
attention. So I never recognized his thirst for travel. I		29	19
didn't expect to find all of those maps near his workplace.		35	23

Skillbuilding

22d Backspace Key

Practice reaching to the Back-space key with your left little finger. Key the sentences, using the backspace key to correct errors.

18 You should be interested in the special items on sale today.

19 If she is going with us, why don't we plan to leave now?

20 Do you desire to continue working on the memo in the future?

21 Did the firm or their neighbors own the autos with problems?

22 Juni, Vec, and Zeb had perfect grades on weekly query exams.

23 Jewel quickly explained to me the big fire hazards involved.

22e Speed Check
1. Take two 1' timings on each paragraph.
2. Take a 3' timing on all paragraphs. Determine *gwam*.

Goal: 17 *gwam*

all letters

	gwam	1'	3'

Most people will agree that we owe it to our children 10 | 4 | 28
to pass the planet on to them in better condition than we 22 | 7 | 32
found it. We must take extra steps just to make the quality 34 | 12 | 36
of living better. 38 | 13 | 37

If we do not change our ways quickly and stop damaging 11 | 16 | 41
our world, it will not be a good place to live. We can save 12 | 21 | 45
the ozone and wildlife and stop polluting the air and water. 35 | 25 | 49

1' | 1 | 2 | 3 | 4 | 5 | 6 | 7 | 8 | 9 | 10 | 11 | 12 |
3' | | 1 | | 2 | | 3 | | 4 | |

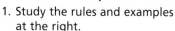

Communication

22f Number Expression

1. Study the rules and examples at the right.
2. In the Open Screen, key the information below at the left margin. Press ENTER as shown.

Your name ENTER

Current date ENTER

Skillbuilders 1, Drill 6
ENTER ENTER

3. Key the sample sentences 24–28. Backspace to correct errors.
4. Save the file as **xx-22f**.

Express as figures

1. **Money amounts** and **percentages, even when appoximate.** Spell out cents and percent except in statistical copy.
   > The 16 percent discount saved me $145; Bill, 95 cents.

2. **Round numbers expressed in millions or higher with their word modifier.**
   > Ms. Ti contributed $3 million.

3. **House numbers** (Except house number One) and street names over ten. If a street name is a number, separate it from the house number with a dash.
   > 1510 Easy Street   One West Ninth Avenue   1592-11th Street

4. **Date followed by a month.** A date preceding the month or standing alone is expressed in figures followed by "d" or "th."
   > June 9, 2001   4th of July   March 3d

5. **Numbers used with nouns.**
   > Volume 1   Chapter 6

24 Ask **Group 1** to read **Chapter 6** of **Book 11** (**Shelf 19, Room 5**).

25 All **six** of us live at **One Bay Road**, not at **126--56th Street**.

26 At **9 a.m.** the owners decided to close from **12 noon** to **1 p.m.**

27 Ms. Vik leaves **June 9**; she returns the **14th or 15th of July.**

28 The **16 percent** discount saves **$115**. A stamp costs **35 cents**.

LESSON 15 | 5 and 0

Warmup

15a

Key each line twice SS.
For a series of capital letters, press CAPS LOCK with the left little finger. Press again to release.

15b Technique
Reinforcement

Reach up or down without moving your hands. Key each line once; repeat drill.

alphabet 1 John Quigley packed the zinnias in twelve large, firm boxes.

1/8 2 Idle Motor 18 at 8 mph and Motor 81 at 8 mph; avoid Motor 1.

caps lock 3 Lily read BLITHE SPIRIT by Noel Coward. I read VANITY FAIR.

easy 4 Did they fix the problem of the torn panel and worn element?

| 1 | 2 | 3 | 4 | 5 | 6 | 7 | 8 | 9 | 10 | 11 | 12 |

adjacent reaches

5 as oil red ask wet opt mop try tree open shred operas treaty
6 were pore dirt stew ruin faster onion alumni dreary mnemonic
7 The opened red hydrants were powerful, fast, and very dirty.

outside reaches

8 pop zap cap zag wasp equip lazy zippers queue opinion quartz
9 zest waste paper exist parquet azalea acquaint apollo apathy
10 The lazy wasp passed the potted azalea on the parquet floor.

New Keys

15c 5 and 0
Key each line once SS.

5 Reach *up* with *left first* finger.

0 Reach *up* with *right fourth* finger.

5

11 5 5f f5 5 5; 5 fans; 5 feet; 5 figs; 5 fobs; 5 furs; 5 flaws
12 5 o'clock; 5 a.m.; 5 p.m.; is 55 or less; buy 55; 5 and 5 is
13 Call Line 555 if 5 fans or 5 bins arrive at Pier 5 by 5 p.m.

0

14 0 0; ;0 0 0; skip 0; plan 0; left 0; is below 0; I scored 0;
15 0 degrees; key 0 and 0; write 00 here; the total is 0 or 00;
16 She laughed at their 0 to 0 score; but ours was 0 to 0 also.

all figures learned

17 I keyed 550 pages for Invoice 05, or 50 more than we needed.
18 Pages 15 and 18 of the program listed 150, not 180, members.
19 On May 10, Rick drove 500 miles to New Mexico in car No. 08.

LESSON 23 | & and : (colon), Proofreaders' Marks

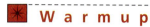

Warmup

23a
Key each line twice SS.

alphabet 1 Roxy waved as she did quick flying jumps on the trapeze bar.

symbols 2 Ryan's--with an A-1 rating--sold Item #146 (for $10) on 2/7.

space bar 3 Mr. Fyn may go to Cape Cod on the bus, or he may go by auto.

easy 4 Susie is busy; may she halt the social work for the auditor?

| 1 | 2 | 3 | 4 | 5 | 6 | 7 | 8 | 9 | 10 | 11 | 12 |

New Keys

23b & and : (colon)
Key each line once SS.

& Shift; then reach up
with *right first* finger.

: (colon) Left shift; then
press key with *right
fourth* finger.

> **& = ampersand:** The
> ampersand is used only
> as part of company
> names.
> **Colon:** Space twice
> after a colon except
> when used within a
> number for time.

& (ampersand)

5 & &j j& & & &; J & J; Haraj & Jay; Moroj & Jax; Torj & Jones
6 Nehru & Unger; Mumm & Just; Mann & Hart; Arch & Jones; M & J
7 Rhye & Knox represent us; Steb & Doy, Firm A; R & J, Firm B.

: (colon)

8 : :; :; : : :; as: for example: notice: To: From: Date:
9 in stock: 8:30; 7:45; Age: Experience: Read: Send: See:
10 Space twice after a colon, thus: To: No.:   Time: Carload:

all symbols learned

11 Consider these companies: J & R, Brand & Kay, Uper & Davis.
12 Memo #88-89 reads as follows: "Deduct 15% of $300, or $45."
13 Bill 32(5)--it got here quite late--from M & N was paid 7/3.

**23c Keyboard
Reinforcement**

Key each line twice; work
for fluency.

double letters

14 Di Bennett was puzzled by drivers exceeding the speed limit.
15 Bill needs the office address; he will cut the grass at ten.
16 Todd saw the green car veer off the street near a tall tree.

figures and symbols

17 Invoice #84 for $672.91, plus $4.38 tax, was due on 5/19/02.
18 Do read Section 4, pages 60-74 and Section 9, pages 198-225.
19 Enter the following: (a) name, (b) address, and (c) tax ID.

New Keys

14c 1 and 8

Key each line once SS.

Note: The digit "1" and the letter "I" have separate values on a computer keyboard. Do not interchange these characters.

1 Reach *up* with *left fourth* finger.

8 Reach *up* with *right second* finger.

Abbreviations: Do not space after a period within an abbreviation, as in Ph.D., U.S., C.O.D., a.m.

1

13 1 1a a1 1 1; 1 and a 1; 1 add 1; 1 aunt; 1 ace; 1 arm; 1 aye
14 1 and 11 and 111; 11 eggs; 11 vats; Set 11A; May 11; Item 11
15 The 11 aces of the 111th Corps each rated a salute at 1 p.m.

8

16 8 8k k8 8 8; 8 kits; ask 8; 8 kites; kick 8; 8 keys; spark 8
17 OK 88; 8 bags; 8 or 88; the 88th; 88 kegs; ask 88; order 888
18 Eight of the 88 cars score 8 or better on our Form 8 rating.

all figures learned

19 She did live at 818 Park, not 181 Park; or was it 181 Clark?
20 Put 1 with 8 to form 18; put 8 with 1 to form 81. Use 1881.
21 On May 1 at 8 a.m., 18 men and 18 women left Gate 8 for Rio.

Skillbuilding

14d Reinforcement

Key each line once; DS between groups. Repeat. Key with accuracy.

figures

22 Our 188 trucks moved 1881 tons on August 18 and December 18.
23 Send Mary 181 No. 188 panes for her home at 8118 Oak Street.
24 The 188 men in 8 boats left Docks 1 and 18 at 1 p.m., May 1.

25 pop was lap pass slaw wool solo swap Apollo wasp load plaque
26 Was Polly acquainted with the equipped jazz player in Texas?
27 The computer is a useful tool; it helps you to perform well.

14e Speed Builder

Set the timer for 1'. Key each sentence as many times as possible.

Goal: to complete each sentence twice in one minute.

28 Did their form entitle them to the land?
29 Did the men in the field signal for us to go?
30 I may pay for the antique bowls when I go to town.
31 The auditor did the work right, so he risks no penalty.
32 The man by the big bush did signal us to turn down the lane.

| 1 | 2 | 3 | 4 | 5 | 6 | 7 | 8 | 9 | 10 | 11 | 12 |

Skillbuilding

23d Speed Builder

Key each line twice; work for fluency.

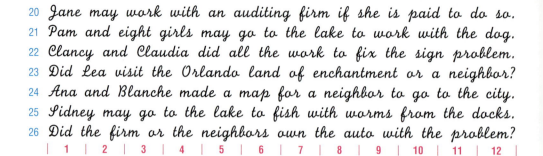

20 Jane may work with an auditing firm if she is paid to do so.
21 Pam and eight girls may go to the lake to work with the dog.
22 Clancy and Claudia did all the work to fix the sign problem.
23 Did Lea visit the Orlando land of enchantment or a neighbor?
24 Ana and Blanche made a map for a neighbor to go to the city.
25 Sidney may go to the lake to fish with worms from the docks.
26 Did the firm or the neighbors own the auto with the problem?

| 1 | 2 | 3 | 4 | 5 | 6 | 7 | 8 | 9 | 10 | 11 | 12 |

23e Speed Check

Key two 1' timed writings on each paragraph; then two 3' writings on both paragraphs; compute *gwam*.

Goals: 1', 20–27 *gwam*
3', 17–24 *gwam*

all letters

	gwam	1'	3'

Is how you judge my work important? It is, of course; | | 11 | 4 | 26
I hope you recognize some basic merit in it. We all expect | | 23 | 8 | 30
to get credit for good work that we conclude. | | 32 | 11 | 33

I want approval for stands I take, things I write, and | | 11 | 14 | 36
work I complete. My efforts, by my work, show a picture of | | 23 | 18 | 41
me; thus, through my work, I am my own unique creation. | | 34 | 22 | 44

1' | 1 | 2 | 3 | 4 | 5 | 6 | 7 | 8 | 9 | 10 | 11 | 12 |
3' | 1 | 2 | 3 | 4 |

Communication

23f Edit Text

1. Read the information about proofreaders' marks.
2. In the Open Screen, key your name, class, and 23f at the left margin. Then key lines 27–32, making the revisions as you key. Use the Backspace key to correct errors.
3. Save as **xx-23f** and print.

Proofreaders' marks are used to identify mistakes in typed or printed text. Learn to apply these commonly used standard proofreaders' marks.

Symbol	Meaning	Symbol	Meaning
～～	Bold	¶	Paragraph
Cap or =	Capitalize	#	Add horizontal space
^	Insert	/ or lc	Lowercase letters
ℓ	Delete	◡	Close up space
⊏	Move to left	～	Transpose
⊐	Move to right	stet	Leave as originally written

27 We miss 50% in life's rewards by refusing to new try things.

28 do it now--today--then tomorrow's load will be 100% lighter.

29 Satisfying work--whether it pays $40 or $400-is the pay off.

30 Avoid mistakes: confusing a #3 has cost thousands.

31 Pleased most with a first-rate job is the person who did it.

32 My wife and/or me mother will except the certifi cate for me.

module 2

Figure and Symbol Keys

OBJECTIVES

* ✳ Key the numeric keys by touch.
* ✳ Use symbol keys correctly.
* ✳ Build keying speed and accuracy.
* ✳ Apply correct number expression.
* ✳ Apply proofreaders' marks.
* ✳ Apply basic Internet skills.

LESSON 14   1 and 8

 W a r m u p

14a

Key each line twice SS.
Line 2: Space once after
a series of brief questions
within a sentence.

alphabet 1	Jessie Quick believed the campaign frenzy would be exciting.
space bar 2	Was it Mary? Helen? Pam? It was a woman; I saw one of them.
3d row 3	We were quietly prepped to write two letters to Portia York.
easy 4	Kale's neighbor works with a tutor when they visit downtown.

| 1 | 2 | 3 | 4 | 5 | 6 | 7 | 8 | 9 | 10 | 11 | 12 |

Skillbuilding

14b High-Frequency Words
The words at the right are
from the 100 most used words.
Key each line once; work for
fluency.

Top 100

5 a an it been copy for his this more no office please service

6 our service than the they up was work all any many thank had

7 business from I know made more not me new of some to program

8 such these two with your about and have like department year

9 by at on but do had in letter most now one please you should

10 their order like also appreciate that there gentlemen letter

11 be can each had information letter may make now only so that

12 them time use which am other been send to enclosed have will

LESSON 24 | Other Symbols

W a r m u p

24a
Key each line twice SS.

alphabet 1 Pfc. Jim Kings covered each of the lazy boxers with a quilt.

figures 2 Do problems 6 to 29 on page 175 before class at 8:30, May 4.

" 3 They read the poems "September Rain" and "The Lower Branch."

easy 4 When did the busy girls fix the tight cowl of the ruby gown?

| 1 | 2 | 3 | 4 | 5 | 6 | 7 | 8 | 9 | 10 | 11 | 12 |

New Keys

24b

Key each pair of lines once SS;
DS between 2-line groups.

Become familiar with
these symbols:

@   at
<   less than
>   greater than
*   asterisk
+   plus sign (use a
    hyphen for minus
    and x for "times")
=   equals
[ ] left and right
    bracket

@   shift; reach *up* with *left third* finger to @

5 @ @s s@ @ @; 24 @ .15; 22 @ .35; sold 2 @ .87; were 12 @ .95
6 You may contact Luke @: LJP@rx.com or fax @ (602) 555-0101.

<   shift; reach *down* with *right second* finger to <
>   shift; reach *down* with *right third* finger to >

7 Can you prove "a > b"? If 28 > 5, then 5a < x. Is a < > b?
8 E-mail Al ajj@crewl.com and Matt mrw10@scxs.com by 9:30 p.m.

*   shift; reach *up* with *right second* finger to *

9 * *k k8* * *; aurelis*; May 7*; both sides*; 250 km.**; aka*
10 Note each *; one * refers to page 29; ** refers to page 307.

+   shift; reach *up* with *right fourth* finger to +

11 + ;+ +; + + +; 2 + 2; A+ or B+; 70+ F. degrees; +xy over +y;
12 The question was 8 + 7 + 51; it should have been 8 + 7 + 15.

=   reach *up* with *right fourth* finger to =

13 = =; = = =; = 4; If 14x = 28, x = 2; if 8x = 16, then x = 2.
14 Change this solution (where it says "= by") to = bx or = BX.

[ ]   reach *up* with *right fourth* finger to [and]

15 Mr. Wing was named. [That's John J. Wing, ex-senator. Ed.]
16 We [Joseph and I] will be in Suite #349; call us @ 555-0102.

These writings may be used as Diagnostic Writings.

Writing 5: 26 *gwam*

gwam 2'

We usually get best results when we know where we are   5

going. Just setting a few goals will help us quietly see what   12

we are doing.   13

Goals can help measure whether we are moving at a good   19

rate or dozing along. You can expect a goal to help you find   25

good results.   26

Writing 6: 28 *gwam*

To win whatever prizes we want from life, we must plan to   6

move carefully from this goal to the next to get the maximum   12

result from our work.   14

If we really want to become skilled in keying, we must   19

come to see that this desire will require of us just a little   26

patience and hard work.   28

Writing 7: 30 *gwam*

Am I an individual person? I'm sure I am; still, in a   5

much, much bigger sense, other people have a major voice in   12

thoughts I think and actions I take.   15

Although we are each a unique person, we all work and   21

play in organized groups of people who do not expect us to   26

dismiss their rules of law and order.   30

2' | 1 | 2 | 3 | 4 | 5 | 6 |

Skillbuilding

24c Rhythm Builder

In the Open Screen, key each line twice; DS between two-line groups.

double letters
17 feel pass mill good miss seem moons cliffs pools green spell
18 Assets are being offered in a stuffy room to two associates.

balanced hand
19 is if of to it go do to is do so if to to the it sign vie to
20 Pamela Fox may wish to go to town with Blanche if she works.

one hand
21 date face ere bat lip sew lion rear brag fact join eggs ever
22 get fewer on; after we look; as we agree; add debt; act fast

combination
23 was for|in the case of|they were|to down|mend it|but pony is
24 They were to be down in the fastest sleigh if you are right.

| 1 | 2 | 3 | 4 | 5 | 6 | 7 | 8 | 9 | 10 | 11 | 12 |

24d Edited Copy

1. Key each line, making the corrections marked with proofreaders' marks.
2. Correct errors using the Backspace key.
3. Save as **xx-24d**.

25 Ask Group 1 to read Chater 6 of Book 11 (Shelf 19, Room 5).

26 All 6 of us live at One Bay road, not at 126-56th Street. *six*

27 AT 9 a.m. the owners decided to close from 12 noon to 1 p.m.

28 Ms. Vik leaves June 9; she returns the 14th or 15th of July.

29 The 16 percent discount saves $115. A stamp costs 35 cents.

30 Elin gave $300,000,000; our gift was only 75 cents. *$3 million* *to charity*

24e Speed Check

1. Key a 1' writing on each paragraph.
2. Key two 3' writings on both paragraphs. Save the timings if desired (**xx24e-t1** and **xx24e-t2**).

	gwam	1'	3'

Why don't we like change very much? Do you think that
just maybe we want to be lazy; to dodge new things; and, as
much as possible, not to make hard decisions?
We know change can and does extend new areas for us to
enjoy, areas we might never have known existed; and to stay
away from all change could curtail our quality of life.

	1'		3'
	11	4	26
	23	8	30
	32	11	33
	11	14	36
	24	18	40
	34	22	44

1'| 1 | 2 | 3 | 4 | 5 | 6 | 7 | 8 | 9 | 10 | 11 | 12 |
3'| 1 | 2 | 3 | 4 |

Communication

24f Composition Revision

1. In the Open Screen, open the file **xx-profile** that you created in Lesson 18.
2. Position the insertion point at the end of the last paragraph. Press ENTER twice.
3. Key an additional paragraph that begins with the following sentence:
   Thank you for allowing me to introduce myself.
4. Finish the paragraph by adding two or more sentences that describe your progress and satisfaction with keyboarding.
5. Correct any mistakes you have made. Click **Save** to resave the document. Print.
6. Mark any mistakes you missed with proofreaders' marks. Revise the document, save, and reprint. Submit to your instructor.

Goal: build staying power
1. Key each paragraph as a
   1' timing.
2. Key a 2' timing on both
   paragraphs.
Note: The dot above text
represents two words.

   all letters

   These writings may
be used as Diagnostic
Writings.

Writing 1: **18 *gwam***   *gwam* 2'

      Why spend weeks with some problem when just a few quiet   6
minutes can help us to resolve it.   9
      If we don't take time to think through a problem, it will   15
swiftly begin to expand in size.   18

Writing 2: **20 *gwam***

      We push very hard in our quest for growth, and we all   5
think that only excellent growth will pay off.   10
      Believe it or not, one can actually work much too hard,   16
be much too zealous, and just miss the mark.   20

Writing 3: **22 *gwam***

      A business friend once explained to me why he was often   6
quite eager to be given some new project to work with.   11
      My friend said that each new project means he has to   16
organize and use the best of his knowledge and his skill.   22

Writing 4: **24 *gwam***

      Don't let new words get away from you. Learn how to spell   6
and pronounce new words and when and how finally to use them.   12
      A new word is a friend, but frequently more. New words   18
must be used lavishly to extend the size of your own word power.   24

2' | 1 | 2 | 3 | 4 | 5 | 6 |

LESSON 25 | Assessment

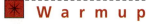

 W a r m u p

25a
Key each line twice SS.

alphabet 1 My wife helped fix a frozen lock on Jacque's vegetable bins.

figures 2 Sherm moved from 823 West 150th Street to 9472--67th Street.

double letters 3 Will Scott attempt to sell his bookkeeping books to Elliott?

easy 4 It is a shame he used the endowment for a visit to the city.

   | 1 | 2 | 3 | 4 | 5 | 6 | 7 | 8 | 9 | 10 | 11 | 12 |

25b Reach Review
Key each line once; repeat.

> **TECHNIQUE TIP**
> Keep arms and hands quiet as you practice the long reaches.

n/y 5 deny many canny tiny nymph puny any puny zany penny pony yen

6 Jenny Nyles saw many, many tiny nymphs flying near her pony.

b/r 7 bran barb brim curb brat garb bray verb brag garb bribe herb

8 Barb Barber can bring a bit of bran and herbs for her bread.

c/e 9 cede neck nice deck dice heck rice peck vice erect mice echo

10 Can Cecil erect a decent cedar deck? He erects nice condos.

n/u 11 nun gnu bun nut pun numb sun nude tuna nub fun null unit gun

12 Eunice had enough ground nuts at lunch; Uncle Launce is fun.

25c Speed Check
Key two 3' writings.
Strive for accuracy.
Goal: 3', 19–27 *gwam*

C all letters

	gwam	3'

The term careers can mean many different things to — 3 | 51

different people. As you know, a career is much more than a — 8 | 55

job. It is the kind of work that a person has through life. — 12 | 59

It includes the jobs a person has over time. It also involves — 16 | 63

how the work life affects the other parts of our life. There — 20 | 67

are as many types of careers as there are people. — 23 | 71

    Almost all people have a career of some kind. A career — 27 | 74

can help us to reach unique goals, such as to make a living — 31 | 79

or to help others. The kind of career you have will affect — 35 | 83

your life in many ways. For example, it can determine where — 39 | 87

you live, the money you make, and how you feel about yourself. — 44 | 91

A good choice can thus help you realize the life you want. — 47 | 95

3' | 1 | 2 | 3 | 4 |

Goal: improve troublesome pairs

Use a controlled rate without pauses.

1 ad add did does dish down body dear dread dabs bad

d/k 2 kid ok kiss tuck wick risk rocks kayaks corks buck

3 Dirk asked Dick to kid Drake about the baked duck.

4 deed deal den led heed made needs delay he she her

e/i 5 kit kiss kiln kiwi kick kilt kind six ribs kill it

6 Abie had neither ice cream nor fried rice in Erie.

7 fib fob fab rib beg bug rob bad bar bed born table

b/v 8 vat vet gave five ever envy never visit weave ever

9 Did Harv key jibe or jive, TV or TB, robe or rove?

10 aft after lift gift sit tot the them tax tutu tyro

t/r 11 for far ere era risk rich rock rosy work were roof

12 In Toronto, Ruth told the truth about her artwork.

13 jug just jury judge juice unit hunt bonus quiz bug

u/y 14 jay joy lay you your only envy quay oily whey body

15 Willy usually does not buy your Yukon art in July.

Drill 6

Goal: build speed

Set the Timer for 1'.

Key each sentence for 1'. Try to complete each sentence twice (20 *gwam* or more). Ignore errors for now.

1 Dian may make cocoa for the girls when they visit.

2 Focus the lens for the right angle; fix the prism.

3 She may suspend work when she signs the torn form.

4 Augment their auto fuel in the keg by the autobus.

5 As usual, their robot did half turns to the right.

6 Pamela laughs as she signals to the big hairy dog.

7 Pay Vivian to fix the island for the eighty ducks.

| 1 | 2 | 3 | 4 | 5 | 6 | 7 | 8 | 9 | 10 |

Drill 7

Goal: build speed

From the columns at the right, choose a gwam goal that is two to three words higher than your best rate. Set the Timer for **Variable** and then either **20"** or **30"**. Try to reach your goal.

	words	30"	20"
1 Did she make this turkey dish?		12	18
2 Blake and Laurie may go to Dubuque.		14	21
3 Signal for the oak sleigh to turn right.		16	24
4 I blame Susie; did she quench the only flame?		18	27
5 She turns the panel dials to make this robot work.		20	30

| 1 | 2 | 3 | 4 | 5 | 6 | 7 | 8 | 9 | 10 |

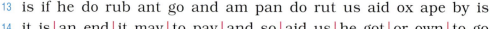

Skillbuilding

25d Rhythm Builder

Key each line once; DS between groups; repeat.

Key with precision and without hesitation.

```
13  is if he do rub ant go and am pan do rut us aid ox ape by is
14  it is|an end|it may|to pay|and so|aid us|he got|or own|to go
15  Did the girl make the ornament with fur, duck down, or hair?

16  us owl rug box bob to man so bit or big pen of jay me age it
17  it|it is|time to go|show them how|plan to go|one of the aims
18  It is a shame they use the autobus for a visit to the field.
    |  1  |  2  |  3  |  4  |  5  |  6  |  7  |  8  |  9  | 10  | 11  | 12  |
```

25e Figure Check

In the Open Screen, key two 1' writings and two 3' writings at a controlled speed.

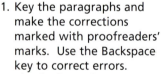

all letters/figures

Goal: 3', 16–24 gwam

gwam 3'

```
              •         4         •         8         •
        Do I read the stock market pages in the news?  Yes; and   4 | 35
      12        •        16         •        20         •
  at about 9 or 10 a.m. each morning, I know lots of excited      8 | 39
    24         •        28         •        32         •
  people are quick to join me.  In fact, many of us zip right    12 | 43
    36         •        40         •        44         •
  to the 3d or 4th part of the paper to see if the prices of     16 | 47
    48         •        52         •        56         •
  our stocks have gone up or down.  Now, those of us who are     19 | 51
    60         •        64         •        68         •
  "speculators" like to "buy at 52 and sell at 60"; while the    23 | 55
    72         •        76         •        80         •
  "investors" among us are more interested in a dividend we      27 | 59
    84         •        88         •        92         •
  may get, say 7 or 8 percent, than in the price of a stock.     31 | 62
  3' |        1        |        2        |        3        |        4        |
```

Communication

25f Edited Copy

1. Key the paragraphs and make the corrections marked with proofreaders' marks. Use the Backspace key to correct errors.
2. Check all number expressions and correct any mistakes that may exist.
3. Save as **xx-25f**.

Last week the healthy heart foundation relased the findings of a study that showed exercise diet and if individuals don't smoke are the major controllable factors that led to a healthy heart. Factors such as heredity can not be controlled. The study included 25 to 65 year old males as well as females.

The study also showed that just taking a walk benefits our health. Those who walked an average of 2 to 3 hours a week were more then 30% less likely to have problems than those who did no exercise.

Drill 2

Goal: strengthen up and down reaches

Keep hands and wrists quiet; fingers well curved in home position; stretch fingers up from home or pull them palmward as needed.

home position
1 Hall left for Dallas; he is glad Jake fed his dog.
2 Ada had a glass flask; Jake had a sad jello salad.
3 Lana Hask had a sale; Gala shall add half a glass.

down reaches
4 Did my banker, Mr. Mavann, analyze my tax account?
5 Do they, Mr. Zack, expect a number of brave women?
6 Zach, check the menu; next, beckon the lazy valet.

up reaches
7 Prue truly lost the quote we wrote for our report.
8 Teresa quietly put her whole heart into her words.
9 There were two hilarious jokes in your quiet talk.

Drill 3

Goal: strengthen individual finger reaches

Rekey troublesome lines.

first finger
1 Bob Mugho hunted for five minutes for your number.
2 Juan hit the bright green turf with his five iron.
3 The frigates and gunboats fought mightily in Java.

second finger
4 Dick said the ice on the creek had surely cracked.
5 Even as we picnicked, I decided we needed to diet.
6 Kim, not Mickey, had rice with chicken for dinner.

third/fourth finger
7 Pam saw Roz wax an aqua auto as Lex sipped a cola.
8 Wally will quickly spell Zeus, Apollo, and Xerxes.
9 Who saw Polly? Zoe Pax saw her; she is quiet now.

Drill 4

Goal: strengthen special reaches

Emphasize smooth stroking. Avoid pauses, but do not reach for speed.

adjacent reaches
1 Falk knew well that her opinions of art were good.
2 Theresa answered her question; order was restored.
3 We join there and walk north to the western point.

direct reaches
4 Barb Nunn must hunt for my checks; she is in debt.
5 In June and December, Irvin hunts in Bryce Canyon.
6 We decided to carve a number of funny human faces.

double letters
7 Anne stopped off at school to see Bill Wiggs cook.
8 Edd has planned a small cookout for all the troop.
9 Keep adding to my assets all fees that will apply.

| 1 | 2 | 3 | 4 | 5 | 6 | 7 | 8 | 9 | 10 |

SKILL BUILDERS 2

 Use the Open Screen for Skill Builders 2. Save each drill as a separate file.

Drill 1

OPPOSITE HAND REACHES

Key at a controlled rate; concentrate on the reaches.

i/e

1 ik is fit it sit laid site like insist still wise coil light
2 ed he ear the fed egg led elf lake jade heat feet hear where
3 lie kite item five aide either quite linear imagine brighter
4 Imagine the aide eating the pears before the grieving tiger.

w/o

5 ws we way was few went wit law with weed were week gnaw when
6 ol on go hot old lot joy odd comb open tool upon money union
7 bow owl word wood worm worse tower brown toward wrote weapon
8 The workers lowered the brown swords toward the wood weapon.

y/t

9 yj my say may yes rye yarn eye lye yap any relay young berry
10 tf at it let the vat tap item town toast right little attire
11 yet toy yogurt typical youth tycoon yacht tympani typewriter
12 Yesterday a young youth typed a cat story on the typewriter.

b/n

13 bf but job fibs orb bow able bear habit boast rabbit brother
14 nj not and one now fun next pony month notice runner quicken
15 bin bran knob born cabin number botany nibble blank neighbor
16 A number of neighbors banked on bunking in the brown cabins.

g/h

17 gag go gee god rig gun log gong cog gig agog gage going gang
18 huh oh hen the hex ash her hash ah hush shah hutch hand ache
19 ugh high ghoul rough ghosts cough night laugh ghee bough ghi
20 Hush; Greg hears rough sounds. Has Hugh laughed or coughed?

r/u

21 row or rid air rap par rye rear ark jar rip nor are right or
22 cut us auk out tutu sun husk but fun cub gun nut mud tug hug
23 rut aura run your rub cure rum our rue cur rug urn true pure
24 Ryan is sure you should pour your food from an urn or cruet.

| 1 | 2 | 3 | 4 | 5 | 6 | 7 | 8 | 9 | 10 | 11 | 12 |

Drill 2

NUMBER SPEED

Take 1' writings; the last number you key when you stop is your approximate *gwam*.

1 and 2 and 3 and 4 and 5 and 6 and 7 and 8 and 9 and 10 and 11 and 12 and 13 and 14 and 15 and 16 and 17 and 18 and 19 and 20 and 21 and 22 and 23 and 24 and 25 and 26 and 27 and

SKILL BUILDERS 1

 Use the Open Screen for Skill Builders 1. Save each drill as a separate file.

Drill 1

Goal: reinforce key locations

Key each line at a comfortable, constant rate; check lines that need more practice; repeat those lines.

Keep

- your eyes on source copy
- your fingers curved, upright
- your wrists low, but not touching
- your elbows hanging loosely
- your feet flat on the floor

A We saw that Alan had an alabaster vase in Alabama.
B My rubber boat bobbed about in the bubbling brook.
C Ceci gave cups of cold cocoa to Rebecca and Rocco.
D Don's dad added a second deck to his old building.
E Even as Ellen edited her document, she ate dinner.
F Our firm in Buffalo has a staff of forty or fifty.
G Ginger is giving Greg the eggs she got from Helga.
H Hugh has eighty high, harsh lights he might flash.
I Irik's lack of initiative is irritating his coach.
J Judge J. J. Jore rejected Jeane and Jack's jargon.
K As a lark, Kirk kicked back a rock at Kim's kayak.
L Lucille is silly; she still likes lemon lollipops.
M Milt Mumm hammered a homer in the Miami home game.
N Ken Linn has gone hunting; Stan can begin canning.
O Jon Soto rode off to Otsego in an old Morgan auto.
P Philip helped pay the prize as my puppy hopped up.
Q Quiet Raquel quit quoting at an exquisite marquee.
R As Mrs. Kerr's motor roared, her red horse reared.
S Sissie lives in Mississippi; Lissa lives in Tulsa.
T Nat told Betty not to tattle on her little sister.
U Ula has a unique but prudish idea on unused units.
V Eva visited every vivid event for twelve evenings.
W We watched as wayworn wasps swarmed by the willow.
X Tex Cox waxed the next box for Xenia and Rex Knox.
Y Ty says you may stay with Fay for only sixty days.
Z Hazel is puzzled about the azure haze; Zack dozes.
alphabet Jacky and Max quickly fought over a sizable prawn.
alphabet Just by maximizing liquids, Chick Prew avoids flu.

| 1 | 2 | 3 | 4 | 5 | 6 | 7 | 8 | 9 | 10 |

TECHNIQUE BUILDERS

Key each line once; DS between groups; repeat.

TECHNIQUE TIP

Concentrate on keeping quiet hands and fingers. Reach directly from the top to bottom rows.

adjacent keys

1 I saw her at an airport at a tropical resort leaving on a cruise.
2 Is assessing potential important in a traditional career program?
3 The boisterous boys were playing on a trampoline near an airport.
4 Three policemen were cruising down that street in Freeport today.

long, direct reach

5 The brave driver swerved to avoid the RV and the boy on the curb.
6 The umpire must check the Brums for number of pitches in one day.
7 The happy bride and groom decided on nuptials preceded by brunch.
8 The nervous mother decided she must keep Marv at a small nursery.

| 1 | 2 | 3 | 4 | 5 | 6 | 7 | 8 | 9 | 10 | 11 | 12 | 13 |

Drill 4

REACH FOR NEW GOALS

1. From the second or third column at the right, choose a goal 2–3 *gwam* higher than your best rate on either straight or statistical copy.

2. Take 1' writings on that sentence; try to finish it the number of times shown at the top of the goal list.

3. If you reach your goal, take 1' writings on the next line. If you don't reach your goal, use the preceding line.

	words	1' timing 6 times gwam	5 times gwam
Do they blame me for the goal?	6	36	30
The 2 men may enamel 17 oboes.	6	36	30
The auditor may handle the problem.	7	42	35
Did the 4 chaps focus the #75 lens?	7	42	35
She did vow to fight for the right name.	8	48	40
He paid 10 men to fix a pen for 3 ducks.	8	48	40
The girl may cycle down to the dormant field.	9	54	45
The 27 girls paid their $9 to go to the lake.	9	54	45
The ensign works with vigor to dismantle the auto.	10	60	50
Bob may work problems 8 and 9; Sid did problem 40.	10	60	50
The form may entitle a visitor to pay for such a kayak.	11	66	55
They kept 7 panels and 48 ivory emblems for 29 chapels.	11	66	55

| 1 | 2 | 3 | 4 | 5 | 6 | 7 | 8 | 9 | 10 | 11 |

Drill 5

IMPROVE CONCENTRATION

Set a right tab at 5.5" for the addresses. Key the Internet addresses in column 2 exactly as they are listed. Accuracy is critical.

The paperless guide to New York City	http://www.mediabridge.com/nyc
A trip to outer space	http://spacelink.msfc.nasa.gov
Search engine	http://webcrawler.com
Government printing office access	http://www.access.gpo.gov/index.html
MarketPlace--corporate information	http://www.mktplace.com
Touchstone's PC-cillin virus scan	http://www.antivirus.com

13d Troublesome Pairs

Key each line once; repeat if time permits.

TECHNIQUE TIP

Keep hands and arms still as you reach up to the third row and down to the first row.

```
t  22  at fat hat sat to tip the that they fast last slat
r  23  or red try ran run air era fair rid ride trip trap
t/r 24  A trainer sprained an arm trying to tame the bear.

m  25  am me my mine jam man more most dome month minimum
n  26  no an now nine once net knee name ninth know never
m/n 27  Many men and women are important company managers.

o  28  on or to not now one oil toil over only solo today
i  29  it is in tie did fix his sit like with insist will
o/i 30  Joni will consider obtaining options to buy coins.

a  31  at an as art has and any case data haze tart smart
s  32  us as so say sat slap lass class just sassy simple
a/s 33  Disaster was averted as the steamer sailed to sea.

e  34  we he ear the key her hear chef desire where there
i  35  it is in tie did fix his sit like with insist will
e/i 36  An expression of gratitude for service is desired.
```

13e Speed Check

1. In the Open Screen, key the paragraphs once SS.
2. Save as **xx-13e**.
3. Take a 1' writing on paragraph 1. Save as **xx-13e-t1**.
4. Take a 1' writing on paragraph 2. Save as **xx-13e-t2**.
5. Print the better 1' writing.
6. Take a 2' writing on both paragraphs. Start over if time permits.

  all letters

Goal: 16 *gwam*

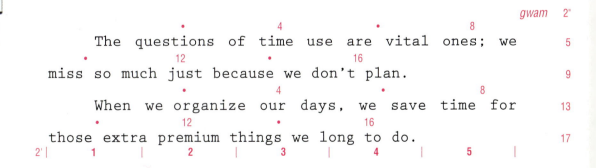

```
                                                              gwam  2"
            •                4          •               8
        The  questions  of  time  use  are  vital  ones;  we      5
    •              12          •              16
miss so much just because we don't plan.                          9
            •                4          •               8
        When  we  organize  our  days,  we  save  time  for       13
    •              12          •              16
those extra premium things we long to do.                         17
2' |      1      |      2      |      3      |      4      |      5      |
```

Drill 6

ASSESS SKILL GROWTH: STRAIGHT COPY

1. Key 1' writings on each paragraph of a timing. Note that paragraphs within a timing increase by two words.

   Goal: to complete each paragraph.

2. Key a 3' timing on the entire writing.

 all letters

To access writings on *MicroPace Pro*, key **W** and the timing number. For example, key **W8** for *Writing 8*.

Timings are also available as Diagnostic Writings in *Keyboarding Pro*.

Writing 8

	1'	3'
Any of us whose target is to achieve success in our professional	13	4
lives will understand that we must learn how to work in harmony	26	8
with others whose paths may cross ours daily.	35	12
We will, unquestionably, work for, with, and beside people, just	13	16
as they will work for, with, and beside us. We will judge them,	26	20
as most certainly they are going to be judging us.	38	24
A lot of people realize the need for solid working relations and	13	28
have a rule that treats others as they, themselves, expect to be	26	33
treated. This seems to be a sound, practical idea for them.	40	37

Writing 9

	1'	3'
I spoke with one company visitor recently; and she was very much	13	4
impressed, she said, with the large amount of work she had noted	26	9
being finished by one of our front office workers.	36	12
I told her how we had just last week recognized this very person	13	16
for what he had done, for output, naturally, but also because of	26	21
its excellence. We know this person has that "magic touch."	38	25
This "magic touch" is the ability to do a fair amount of work in	13	29
a fair amount of time. It involves a desire to become ever more	26	34
efficient without losing quality--the "touch" all workers should	39	38
have.	40	38

Writing 10

	1'	3'
Isn't it great just to untangle and relax after you have keyed a	13	4
completed document? Complete, or just done? No document is	25	8
quite complete until it has left you and passed to the next step.	38	13
There are desirable things that must happen to a document before	13	17
you surrender it. It must be read carefully, first of all, for	26	22
meaning to find words that look right but aren't. Read word for	39	26
word.	40	26
Check all figures and exact data, like a date or time, with your	13	31
principal copy. Make sure format details are right. Only then,	26	35
print or remove the work and scrutinize to see how it might look	39	39
to a recipient.	42	40

1'	1	2	3	4	5	6	7	8	9	10	11	12	13
3'		1			2			3			4		

LESSON 13 | Review

W a r m u p

13a
Key each line twice SS
(slowly, then faster).

alphabet 1 Bev quickly hid two Japanese frogs in Mitzi's box.

shift 2 Jay Nadler, a Rotary Club member, wrote Mr. Coles.

, (comma) 3 Jay, Ed, and I paid for plates, knives, and forks.

easy 4 Did the amendment name a city auditor to the firm?

| 1 | 2 | 3 | 4 | 5 | 6 | 7 | 8 | 9 | 10 |

Skillbuilding

13b Rhythm Builders
Key each line once SS.

word-level response: key short, familiar words as units

5 is to for do an may work so it but an with them am

6 Did they mend the torn right half of their ensign?

7 Hand me the ivory tusk on the mantle by the bugle.

letter-level response: key more difficult words letter by letter

8 only state jolly zest oil verve join rate mop card

9 After defeat, look up; gaze in joy at a few stars.

10 We gazed at a plump beaver as it waded in my pool.

combination response: use variable speed; your fingers will let you feel the difference

11 it up so at for you may was but him work were they

12 It is up to you to get the best rate; do it right.

13 This is Lyn's only date to visit their great city.

| 1 | 2 | 3 | 4 | 5 | 6 | 7 | 8 | 9 | 10 |

13c Keyboard Reinforcement

Key each line once; fingers well curved, wrists low; avoid punching keys with 3rd and 4th fingers.

p 14 Pat appears happy to pay for any supper I prepare.

x 15 Knox can relax; Alex gets a box of flax next week.

v 16 Vi, Ava, and Viv move ivy vines, leaves, or stems.

' 17 It's a question of whether they can't or won't go.

? 18 Did Jan go? Did she see Ray? Who paid? Did she?

. 19 Ms. E. K. Nu and Lt. B. A. Walz had the a.m. duty.

" 20 "Who are you?" he asked. "I am," I said, "Marie."

; 21 Find a car; try it; like it; work a price; buy it.

GUIDED WRITING: IMPROVE SPEED/ ACCURACY

Key as 1' guided writings, working for either speed or control.

Optional: Key as a 3' writing.

To access writings on *MicroPace Pro*, key **W** and the timing number. For example, key **W11** for Writing 11.

Writing 11

gwam 3'

Anyone who expects some day to find an excellent job should	4	34
begin now to learn the value of accuracy. To be worth anything,	8	38
completed work must be correct, without question. Naturally, we	13	43
realize that the human aspect of the work equation always raises	17	47
the prospect of errors; but we should understand that those same	20	51
errors can be found and fixed. Every completed job should carry	26	56
at least one stamp; the stamp of pride in work that is exemplary.	30	60

Writing 12

No question about it: Many personal problems we face today	4	34
arise from the fact that we earthlings have never been very wise	8	38
consumers. We haven't consumed our natural resources well; as a	13	43
result, we have jeopardized much of our environment. We excused	17	47
our behavior because we thought that our stock of most resources	20	51
had no limit. So, finally, we are beginning to realize just how	26	56
indiscreet we were; and we are taking steps to rebuild our world.	30	60

Writing 13

When I see people in top jobs, I know I'm seeing people who	4	34
sell. I'm not just referring to employees who labor in a retail	8	38
outlet; I mean those people who put extra effort into convincing	13	43
others to recognize their best qualities. They, themselves, are	17	47
the commodity they sell; and their optimum tools are appearance,	20	51
language, and personality. They look great, they talk and write	26	56
well; and, with candid self-confidence, they meet you eye to eye.	30	60

3' | 1 | 2 | 3 | 4 |

12d Speed Builder

1. Practice each line as fast as possible to build stroking speed.
2. Save as **xx-L12**. (Substitute your initials for *xx*.)

> **TECHNIQUE TIP**
>
> Keep hands quiet; keep fingers curved and upright.

12e Speed Check

1. In the Open Screen, key both paragraphs using wordwrap. Work for smooth, continuous stroking, not speed.
2. Save as **xx-12e**. Substitute your initials for *xx*.
3. Take a 1' writing on paragraph 1. Save as **xx-12e-t1**.
4. Repeat step 3 using paragraph 2. Save as **xx-12e-t2**.
5. Set the Timer for 2'. Take a 2' writing on both paragraphs. Save as **xx-12e-t3**.

 all letters

Goal: 16 *wam*

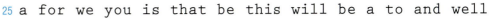

25 a for we you is that be this will be a to and well
26 as our with I or a to by your form which all would
27 new year no order they so new but now year who may

28 This is Lyn's only date to visit their great city.
29 I can send it to your office at any time you wish.
30 She kept the fox, owls, and fowl down by the lake.

31 Harriette will cook dinner for the swimming teams.
32 Annette will call at noon to give us her comments.
33 Johnny was good at running and passing a football.
| 1 | 2 | 3 | 4 | 5 | 6 | 7 | 8 | 9 | 10 |

Copy Difficulty

What factors determine whether copy is difficult or easy? Research shows that difficulty is influenced by syllables per word, characters per word, and percent of familiar words. Carefully controlling these three factors ensures that speed and accuracy scores are reliable—that is, increased scores reflect increased skill.

In Level 1, all timings are easy. Note "E" inside the triangle at left of the timing. Easy timings contain an average of 1.2 syllables per word, 5.1 characters per word, and 90 percent familiar words. Easy copy is suitable for the beginner who is mastering the keyboard.

gwam 2'

There should be no questions, no doubt, about	5	35
the value of being able to key; it's just a matter	10	40
of common sense that today a pencil is much too slow.	15	45
Let me explain. Work is done on a keyboard	19	49
three to six times faster than other writing and	24	54
with a product that is a prize to read. Don't you	29	59
agree?	30	60

2' | 1 | 2 | 3 | 4 | 5 |

These writings may be used as Diagnostic Writings

To access writings on *MicroPace Pro*, key **W** and the timing number. For example, key **W14** for Writing 14.

Writing 14

	gwam
	1' | 3'

What do you expect when you travel to a foreign country? | 12 | 4
Quite a few people realize that one of the real joys of | 23 | 8
traveling is to get a brief glimpse of how others think, work, | 36 | 12
and live. | 40 | 12

The best way to enjoy a different culture is to learn as | 11 | 16
much about it as you can before you leave home. Then you can | 24 | 20
concentrate on being a good guest rather than trying to find | 36 | 24
local people who can meet your needs. | 44 | 27

Writing 15

	gwam
	1' | 3'

What do you enjoy doing in your free time? Health experts | 12 | 4
tell us that far too many people choose to be lazy rather than | 24 | 8
to be active. The result of that decision shows up in our | 36 | 12
weight. | 37 | 13

Working to control what we weigh is not easy, and seldom | 12 | 16
can it be done quickly. However, it is quite important if our | 24 | 21
weight exceeds what it should be. Part of the problem results | 37 | 25
from the amount and type of food we eat. | 44 | 27

If we want to look fit, we should include exercise as a | 11 | 31
substantial part of our weight loss plan. Walking at least | 23 | 35
thirty minutes each day at a very fast rate can make a big | 35 | 39
difference both in our appearance and in the way we feel. | 47 | 42

Writing 16

	gwam
	1' | 3'

Doing what we like to do is quite important; however, | 10 | 4
liking what we have to do is equally important. As you ponder | 23 | 8
both of these concepts, you may feel that they are the same, | 36 | 12
but they are not the same. | 41 | 14

If we could do only those things that we prefer to do, the | 12 | 18
chances are that we would do them exceptionally well. Generally, | 25 | 22
we will take more pride in doing those things we like doing, | 37 | 26
and we will not quit until we get them done right. | 47 | 29

We realize, though, that we cannot restrict the things | 11 | 33
that we must do just to those that we want to do. Therefore, | 23 | 37
we need to build an interest in and an appreciation of all the | 36 | 41
tasks that we must do in our positions. | 44 | 44

1'	1	2	3	4	5	6	7	8	9	10	11	12
3'		1			2			3			4	

LESSON 12 | Review

Warmup

12a
Key each line twice SS (slowly, then faster).

alphabet 1 Jack won five quiz games; Brad will play him next.

q 2 Quin Racq quickly and quietly quelled the quarrel.

z 3 Zaret zipped along sizzling, zigzag Arizona roads.

easy 4 Did he hang the sign by the big bush at the lake?

| 1 | 2 | 3 | 4 | 5 | 6 | 7 | 8 | 9 | 10 |

Skillbuilding

12b New Key Review
Key each line once; DS between groups; work for smoothness, not for speed.

b/f 5 bf bf fab fab ball bib rf rf rib rib fibs bums bee

6 Did Buffy remember that he is a brass band member?

z/y 7 za za zag zig zip yj yj jay eye day lazy hazy zest

8 Liz amazed us with the zesty pizza on a lazy trip.

q/u 9 qa qa quo qt. quit quay quad quarm que uj jug quay

10 Where is Quito? Qatar? Boqueirao? Quebec? Quilmes?

v/m 11 vf vf valve five value mj mj ham mad mull mass vim

12 Vito, enter the words vim, vivace, and avar; save.

all 13 I faced defeat; only reserves saved my best crews.

14 In my opinion, I need to rest in my reserved seat.

all 15 Holly created a red poppy and deserves art awards.

16 My pump averages a faster rate; we get better oil.

12c Reach Review
Key each line once; work for smooth, unhurried keying.

de/ed 17 ed fed led deed dell dead deal sled desk need seed

18 Dell dealt with the deed before the dire deadline.

ol/lo 19 old tolls doll solo look sole lost love cold stole

20 Old Ole looked for the long lost olive oil lotion.

op/po 21 pop top post rope pout port stop opal opera report

22 Stop to read the top opera opinion report to Opal.

TECHNIQUE TIP
Keep fingers curved and body aligned properly.

we/ew 23 we few wet were went wears weather skews stew blew

24 Working women wear sweaters when weather dictates.

Writing 17

gwam 1' 3'

Many people like to say just how lucky a person is when he or she succeeds in doing something well. Does luck play a large role in success? In some cases, it might have a small effect.

Being in the right place at the right time may help, but hard work may help far more than luck. Those who just wait for luck should not expect quick results and should realize luck may never come.

Writing 18

gwam 1' 3'

New golfers must learn to zero in on just a few social rules. Do not talk, stand close, or move around when another person is hitting. Be ready to play when it is your turn.

Take practice swings in an area away from other people. Let the group behind you play through if your group is slow. Do not rest on your club on the green when waiting your turn.

Set your other clubs down off the green. Leave the green quickly when done; update your card on the next tee. Be sure to leave the course in good condition. Always have a good time.

Writing 19

gwam 1' 3'

Do you know how to use time wisely? If you do, then its proper use can help you organize and run a business better. If you find that your daily problems tend to keep you from planning properly, then perhaps you are not using time well. You may find that you spend too much time on tasks that are not important. Plan your work to save valuable time.

A firm that does not plan is liable to run into trouble. A small firm may have trouble planning. It is important to know just where the firm is headed. A firm may have a fear of learning things it would rather not know. To say that planning is easy would be absurd. It requires lots of thinking and planning to meet the expected needs of the firm.

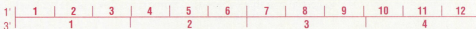

11d Technique Builder

Key each line once; DS between groups.

TECHNIQUE TIP

Press CAPS LOCK to capitalize several letters. Press it again to toggle CAPS LOCK off.

enter: key smoothly without looking at fingers

21 Make the return snappily
22 and with assurance; keep
23 your eyes on your source
24 data; maintain a smooth,
25 constant pace as you key.

space bar: use down-and-in motion

26 us me it of he an by do go to us if or so am ah el
27 Have you a pen? If so, print "Free to any guest."

caps lock: press to toggle it on or off

28 Use ALL CAPS for items such as TO: FROM: SUBJECT.
29 Did Kristin mean Kansas City, MISSOURI, or KANSAS?

11e Speed Check

1. In the Open Screen, key all paragraphs. Work for smooth, continuous stroking, not speed.
2. Save as **xx-11e**. Substitute your initals for *xx*.
3. Take a 2' writing on all paragraphs.

Goal: 16 *gwam*

To determine gross-words-a-minute (*gwam*) rate for 2':
Follow these steps if you are *not* using the Timer in the Open Screen.

1. Note the figure at the end of the last line completed.

2. For a partial line, note the figure on the scale direcly below the point at which you stopped keying.

3. Add these two figures to determine the total gross words a minute (*gwam*) you keyed.

					gwam	2'
Have we thought of communication as a kind					4	31
of war that we wage through each day?					8	35
When we think of it that way, good language					12	39
would seem to become our major line of attack.					17	44
Words become muscle; in a normal exchange or in					22	49
a quarrel, we do well to realize the power of words.					27	54

11f Enrichment

1. Go to the Skillbuilding Workshop 1, Drill 1, page 31. Choose 6 letters that cause you difficulty. Key each line twice. Put a checkmark beside the lines in the book so that you know you have practiced them.

2. Save the drill as **xx-11f**. Substitute your initials for xx.

INTERNET ACTIVITIES

 Activity 1

Open Web Browser

Know your Browser

Knowing your browser includes opening the browser, opening a Web site, and getting familiar with the browser toolbar. You will also learn to set a bookmark at a favorite Web site.

Word users can quickly access the Internet while in *Word* by using the Web toolbar.

1. Display the Web toolbar by right-clicking on any toolbar and then choosing **Web** from the list of choices.

2. Open your Web browser by clicking the **Start Page** button on the Web toolbar. The Web page you have designated as your Home or Start Page displays.

Start Page

D r i l l   1

1. Begin a new *Word* document.
2. Display the Web toolbar.
3. Click the **Start Page** button to open your Web browser.

Open Web Site

With the Web browser open, click **Open** or **Open Page** from the **File** menu (or click the **Open** button if it is available on your browser's toolbar). Key the Web address (e.g., http://www.weather.com) and click **Open**. The Web site displays.

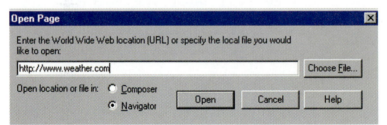

Shortcut: Click inside the Location or Address entry box, key the web address, and press ENTER.

A **Web address** or site—commonly called the *URL* or *Uniform Resource Locator*—is composed of one or more domains separated by periods: http://www.house.gov/.

As you move from left to right in the address, each domain is larger than the previous one. In the Web address above, *gov* (United State government) is larger than *house* (House of Representatives). Other domains include educational institutions (.edu), commercial organizations (.com), military sites (.mil), and other organizations (.org).

A Web address may also include a directory path and filenames separated by slashes. In the address below, the Web document named *news* resides at this site. http://ur.mstate.edu/news/

LESSON 11 | Review

Warmup

11a
Key each line twice SS
(slowly, then faster).

alphabet	1	Zeb had Jewel quickly give him five or six points.
" (quote)	2	Can you spell "chaos," "bias," "bye," and "their"?
y	3	Ty Clay may envy you for any zany plays you write.
easy	4	Did he bid on the bicycle, or did he bid on a map?

| 1 | 2 | 3 | 4 | 5 | 6 | 7 | 8 | 9 | 10 |

Skillbuilding

11b Keyboard Reinforcement

Key each line once; repeat the drill to increase fluency.

5 za za zap az az maze zoo zip razz zed zax zoa zone
6 Liz Zahl saw Zoe feed the zebra in an Arizona zoo.

7 yj yj jy jy joy lay yaw say yes any yet my try you
8 Why do you say that today, Thursday, is my payday?

9 xs xs sax ox box fix hex ax lax fox taxi lox sixes
10 Roxy, you may ask Jay to fix any tax sets for you.

11 qa qa aqua quail quit quake quid equal quiet quart
12 Did Enrique quietly but quickly quell the quarrel?

13 fv fv five lives vow ova van eve avid vex vim void
14 Has Vivi, Vada, or Eva visited Vista Valley Farms?

> **TECHNIQUE TIP**
> Work for smoothness, not for speed.

11c Speed Builders
Key each balanced-hand line twice, as quickly as you can.

15 is to for do an may work so it but an with them am
16 am yam map aid zig yams ivy via vie quay cob amend

17 to do is for an may work so it but am an with them
18 for it|for it|to the|to the|do they|do they|do it

19 Pamela may go to the farm with Jan and a neighbor.
20 Rod and Ty may go by the lake if they go downtown.

| 1 | 2 | 3 | 4 | 5 | 6 | 7 | 8 | 9 | 10 |

Drill 2

Open the following Web sites. Identify the high-level domain for each site.

1. http://www.weather.com _____
2. http://fbla-pbl.org _____
3. http://www.army.mil _____
4. http://www.senate.gov _____

Drill 3

Open the following Web sites and identify the filenames.

1. http://www.cnn.com/TRAVEL/ _____
2. http://espn.go.com/ncaa/ _____
3. http://www.usps.gov/ctc/welcome.htm _____

Explore the Browser's Toolbar

The browser's toolbar is very valuable when surfing the Internet. Become familiar with your browser's toolbar by studying the screen. Browsers may vary slightly.

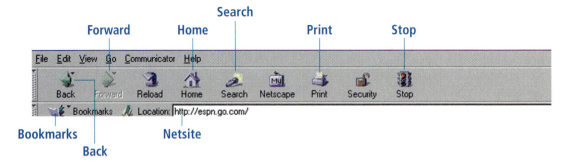

Netsite entry box	Displays the active URL or Web site address.
Back	Moves to Web sites or pages visited since opening the browser.
Forward	Moves forward to sites visited prior to using the Back button. (The Forward button is ghosted if the Back button has not been used.)
Print	Prints a Web page.
Home	Returns to the Web page designated as the Home or Start Page.
Stop	Stops computer's search for a Web site.
Search	Opens one of the Internet search engines.
Bookmarks	Moves to the list of Web sites marked for easy access.

Drill 4

1. Open the following Web sites:
   a. http://nike.com
   b. http://realage.com
   c. http://mapquest.com
   d. A site of your choice
2. Click the **Back** button twice. The_____Web site displays.
3. Click the **Forward** button once. The_____Web site displays.
4. Print the active Web page.

10d  " (quotation mark) and TAB

Key each line once; repeat.

" Shift; then reach to " with *right fourth* finger.

TAB Reach up with *left fourth* finger.

" (quotation mark)

20 "; "; " " "lingo" "bugs" "tennies" I like "malts."
21 "I am not," she said, "going." I just said, "Oh?"

tab key

22   The tab key is used for indenting paragraphs
and aligning columns.
23   Tabs that are set by the software are called
default tabs, which are usually a half inch.

all reaches learned

24   The expression "I give you my word," or put another
25 way, "Take my word for it," is just a way I can say, "I
26 prize my name; it clearly stands in back of my words."
27 I offer "honor" as collateral.

Skillbuilding

10e Reinforcement

Follow the standard directions on page 8. Key each line twice; DS between groups.

10f Speed Check

Take two 1' writings of paragraph 2 in the Open Screen. Save as **xx-10e-t1** and **xx-10e-t2**.
Goal: 15 *wam*

tab 28   Strike the tab key and begin the line without a pause
to maintain fluency.

29   She said that this is the lot to be sent; I
agreed with her.

30   Strike Tab before starting to key a timed
writing so that the first line is indented.

gwam 1'

Tab → All of us work for progress, but it is not   8
always easy to analyze "progress." We work hard   18
for it; but, in spite of some really good efforts, 28
we may fail to receive just exactly the response we 39
want.   40
Tab → When this happens, as it does to all of us,   9
it is time to cease whatever we are doing, have   18
a quiet talk with ourselves, and face up to the   28
questions about our limited progress. How can we   38
do better?   40

| 1 | 2 | 3 | 4 | 5 | 6 | 7 | 8 | 9 | 10 |

Bookmark a Favorite Web Site

When readers put a book aside, they insert a bookmark to mark the place. Internet users also add bookmarks to mark their favorite Web sites or sites of interest for browsing later.

To add a bookmark:

1. Open the desired Web site.
2. Click **Bookmarks** and then **Add Bookmark**. (Browsers may vary on location and name of Bookmark button.)

To use a bookmark:

1. Click **Bookmarks** (or **Communicator**, **Favorites**, or **Window Bookmarks**).
2. Select the desired bookmark. Click or double-click, depending on your browser. The desired Web site displays.

Drill 5

1. Open these favorite Web sites and bookmark them on your browser.

   a. http://www.weather.com

   b. http://www.cnn.com

   c. http://ask.com

   d. Key the Web address of a city you would like to visit (destin.com)

2. Use the bookmarks to go to the following Web sites to find answers to the questions shown.

   a. The Weather Channel—What is today's temperature in your city? _____

   b. CNN—What is today's top news story? _____

   c. Ask Jeeves. Ask a question; then find the answer. _____

   d. City Web site you bookmarked—Find one attraction in the city to visit. _____

Activity 2

Set up e-mail addresses

Electronic mail

Electronic mail or **e-mail** refers to electronic messages sent by one computer user to another computer user. To be able to send or receive e-mail, you must have an e-mail address, an e-mail program, and access to the Internet or an intranet (in-house network).

Many search engines such as Excite, Google, Lycos, Hotbot and others provide free e-mail via their Web sites. These e-mail programs allow users to set up an e-mail address and then send and retrieve e-mail messages. To set up an account and obtain an e-mail address, the user must (1) agree to the terms of agreements, (2) complete an online registration form, and (3) compose an e-mail name and password.

Drill 1

1. Click the Search button on the browser's toolbar. Click a search engine that offers free e-mail.

2. Click **Free E-mail** or **Mail**. (Terms will vary.)

3. Read the Terms of Agreement and accept.

4. Enter an e-mail name. This name will be the login-name portion of your e-mail address.

5. Enter a password for your e-mail account. For security reasons, do not share your password, do not leave it where others can use it, and avoid choosing pet names or birth dates.

6. Review the entire registration form and submit it. You will be notified immediately that your e-mail account has been established. (If your e-mail name is already in use by someone else, you may be instructed to choose a different name before your account can be established.)

LESSON 10 | Z, Y, Quotation Mark, Tab

Warmup

10a

Key each line twice.

all letters	1	Quill owed those back taxes after moving to Japan.
spacing	2	Didn't Vi, Sue, and Paul go? Someone did; I know.
q/v/m	3	Marv was quite quick to remove that mauve lacquer.
easy	4	Lana is a neighbor; she owns a lake and an island.

New Keys

10b z and y

Key each line once; repeat.

z Reach *down* with *left fourth* finger.

y Reach *up* with *right first* finger.

z

5 za za zap zap zing zig zag zoo zed zip zap zig zed

6 doze zeal zero haze jazz zone zinc zing size ozone

7 ooze maze doze zoom zarf zebus daze gaze faze adze

y

8 y yj yj jay jay hay hay lay nay say days eyes ayes

9 yj ye yet yen yes cry dry you rye sty your fry wry

10 ye yen bye yea coy yew dye yaw lye yap yak yon any

all reaches learned

11 Did you say Liz saw any yaks or zebus at your zoo?

12 Relax; Jake wouldn't acquire any favorable rights.

13 Has Mazie departed? Tex, Lu, and I will go alone.

10c **Reach Review**

Key each line once. DS between groups. Repeat.

direct reach	14	Cecilia brings my jumbo umbrella to every concert.
	15	John and Kim recently brought us an old art piece.
	16	I built a gray brick border around my herb garden.

adjacent reach	17	sa ui hj gf mn vc ew uy re io as lk rt jk df op yu
	18	In Ms. Lopez' opinion, the opera was really great.
	19	Polly and I were joining Walker at the open house.

Send E-mail Message

To send an e-mail message, you must have the address of the computer user you want to write. Business cards, letterheads, directories, etc., now include e-mail addresses. Often a telephone call is helpful in obtaining e-mail addresses. An e-mail address includes the user's login name followed by @ and the domain (sthomas@yahoo.com)

Creating an e-mail message is quite similar to preparing a memo. The e-mail header includes TO, FROM, and SUBJECT. Key the e-mail address of the recipient on the TO line, and compose a subject line that concisely describes the theme of your message. Your e-mail address will automatically display on the FROM line.

Drill 2

1. Open the search engine used to set up your e-mail account. Click **E-mail** or **Mail**. (Terms will vary.)

2. Enter your e-mail name and password when prompted.

E-mail Message 1

3. Enter the e-mail address of your instructor or another student. Compose a brief message describing the city you would like to visit. Mention one of the city's attractions (from Activity 1, Drill 5). Include a descriptive subject line. Send the message.

E-mail Message 2

4. Enter your e-mail address. The subject is **Journal Entry for March 29, 200-**. Compose a message to show your reflections on how keyboarding is useful to you. Share your progress in the course and your plan for improving this week. Send the message.

Respond to Messages

Replying to e-mail messages

Reading one's e-mail messages and responding promptly are important rules of netiquette (etiquette for the Internet). However, avoid responding too quickly to sensitive situations.

Forwarding e-mail messages

Received e-mail messages are often shared or forwarded to other e-mail users. Be sure to seek permission from the sender of the message before forwarding it to others.

Drill 3

1. Open your e-mail account if it is not open.

2. Read your e-mail messages and respond immediately and appropriately to any e-mail messages received from your instructor or fellow students. Click **Reply** to answer the message.

3. Forward the e-mail message titled *Journal Entry for March 29, 200-* to your instructor.

4. Delete all read messages.

Attach a Document to an E-mail Message

Electronic files can be attached to an e-mail message and sent to another computer electronically. Recipients of attached documents can transfer these documents to their computers and then open them for use.

Drill 4

1. Open your e-mail account if it is not open.

2. Create an e-mail message to your instructor that states your homework is attached. The subject line should include the specific homework assignment (**xx-profile**, for example).

3. Attach the file by clicking **Attach**. Use the browser to locate the homework assignment. (E-mail programs may vary.)

4. Send the e-mail message with the attached file.

9d v and ' (apostrophe)

Key each line once; repeat.

v Reach *down* with *left first* finger.

' Reach to ' with *right fourth* finger.

Apostrophe: The apostrophe shows (1) omission (as Rob't for Robert or it's for it is) or (2) possession when used with nouns (as Joe's hat).

v

20 v vf vf vie vie via via vim vat vow vile vale vote
21 vf vf ave vet ova eve vie dive five live have lave
22 cove dove over aver vivas hive volt five java jive

' (apostrophe)

23 '; '; it's it's Rod's; it's Bo's hat; we'll do it.
24 We don't know if it's Lee's pen or Norma's pencil.
25 It's ten o'clock; I won't tell him that he's late.

all reaches learned

26 It's Viv's turn to drive Iva's van to Ava's house.
27 Qua, not Vi, took the jet; so did Cal. Didn't he?
28 Wasn't Fae Baxter a judge at the post garden show?

Skillbuilding

9e Reinforcement
1. Follow the standard Open Screen directions on page 8.
2. Key each line twice; DS between groups. Strive to increase speed.

v/?
29 Viola said she has moved six times in five months.
30 Does Dave live on Vine Street? Must he leave now?

q/?
31 Did Viv vote? Can Paque move it? Could Val dive?
32 Didn't Raquel quit Carl Quent after their quarrel?

direct reach
33 Fred told Brice that the junior class must depart.
34 June and Hunt decided to go to that great musical.

double letter
35 Harriette will cook dinner for the swimming teams.
36 Bill's committee meets in an accounting classroom.

9f Speed Check
Take two 1' writings on the paragraph. Save the timings as **xx-9e-t1** and **xx-9e-t2**, substituting your initials for *xx*.
Goal: 14 *wam*

```
                      .        4          .        8           .
We must be able to express our thoughts with ease
         .          12         .         16         .          20
if we desire to find success in the business world.
      .         24            .       28
It is there that sound ideas earn cash.
```

 **Activity 3**

Explore search engines

To find information on the World Wide Web (WWW), the best place to start is often a search engine. Search engines are used to locate specific information. Just a few examples of search engines are AltaVista, Excite, Google, AskJeeves, Lycos, and Yahoo.

 To go to a search engine, click on the **Search** button on your Web browser. (Browsers vary.)

Drill

1. Go to the search engines on your browser. Click on the first search engine. Browse the hyperlinks available such as Maps, People Finder, News, Weather, Stock Quotes, Sports, Games, etc. Click each search engine and explore the hyperlinks.

2. Conduct the following search using Dogpile, a multithreaded search engine that searches multiple databases;
   a. Open the Web site for Dogpile (http://www.dogpile. com).
   b. In the Search entry box, key the keywords **American Psychological Association** publications; click **Fetch**.

3. Pick two of the following topics and search for each using three of your browser's search engines. Look over the first ten results you get from each search. Which search engine gave you the greatest number of promising results for each topic?

aerobics	antivirus software	career change
censorship	college financing	teaching tolerance

 Activity 4

Search Yellow Pages

Searching the Yellow Pages for information on businesses and services is commonplace, both in business and at home. Let your computer do the searching for you the next time. Several search engines provide a convenient hyperlink to the Yellow Pages.

Drill

1. Click the **Search** button in your Web browser. Browse the search engines to locate the hyperlinks for the Yellow Pages; click to open this valuable site.

2. Determine a city that you would like to visit. Assume you will need overnight accommodations. Use the Yellow Pages to find a listing of hotels in this city.

3. Your best friend lives in (*you provide the city*); you want to send him/her flowers. Find a listing of florists in this city.

4. You create a third scenario and find listings.

LESSON 9 | Q, M, V, Apostrophe

Warmup

9a
Key each line twice.

all letters	1	Lex gripes about cold weather; Fred is not joking.
space bar	2	Is it Di, Jo, or Al? Ask Lt. Coe, Bill; he knows.
easy	3	I did rush a bushel of cut corn to the sick ducks.
easy	4	He is to go to the Tudor Isle of England on a bus.

New Keys

9b q and m
Key each line once; repeat.

q Reach *up* with *left fourth* finger.

q

5 q qa qa quad quad quaff quant queen quo quit quick

6 qa qu qa quo quit quod quid quip quads quote quiet

7 quite quilts quart quill quakes quail quack quaint

m

8 m mj mj jam man malt mar max maw me mew men hem me

9 m mj ma am make male mane melt meat mist amen lame

10 malt meld hemp mimic tomb foam rams mama mire mind

m Reach *down* with *right first* finger.

all reaches learned

11 Quin had some quiet qualms about taming a macaque.

12 Jake Coxe had questions about a new floor program.

13 Max was quick to join the big reception for Lidia.

9c New Key Review
Key each line once for control. DS and repeat the drill.

| m/x | 14 | me men ma am jam am lax, mix jam; the hem, six men |
| | 15 | Emma Max expressed an aim to make a mammoth model. |

| q/u | 16 | qa qu aqua aqua quit quit quip quite pro quo squad |
| | 17 | Did Quin make a quick request to take the Qu exam? |

| g/n | 18 | fg gn gun gun dig dig nag snag snag sign grab grab |
| | 19 | Georgia hung a sign in front of the union for Gib. |

Activity 5   Map a trip

Determining the route to your destination city is most important in ensuring a pleasant journey. The printed atlas is a valuable tool for mapping a trip; however, with today's technology, we can map our trips electronically using the Maps hyperlinks provided by several search engines. This invaluable site will search for the specific route you identify and provide you an overview map and turn-by-turn maps with text.

Drill

1. Click the **Search** button in your Web browser. Browse the search engines to locate the hyperlinks for *Maps*; click to open.

2. Your destination city is Asheville, North Carolina. Enter your city and state as the starting point. Search for a turn-by-turn map with text. Print the directions.

    What is the total distance? _____ What is the estimated time? _____

3. You are having a party and need to give several guests directions to your home. Using the Excite search engine, go to *Maps* and choose *Map a U.S. Address* to search for directions to your home. Enter your street address, city, state, and ZIP. Print and trim the map to fit in your party invitation.

4. Use *Maps* from the AltaVista search engine to create a map of your city. Use the *Fancy Features* and enter your phone number. Print the map.

Activity 6   Use a comprehensive search engine

Using a comprehensive search engine can be very helpful in locating various information quickly. The All-in-One Web site (http://www.AllOneSearch.com) is a compilation of various search tools found on the Internet. Search tools include various categories, such as *People*, *News/Weather*, *Desk Reference*, and *Other Interesting Searches/Services*.

Drill

1. Open the All-in-One Web site (http://www.AllOneSearch.com). Browse the various categories and the many search tools within the categories.

2. From the *People* category:

    a. Use BigFoot to find the e-mail address for (*provide a name*).

    b. Use Ahoy! to find the home page for (*provide a name*).

3. From the *News/Weather* category:

    a. Use Pathfinder Weather Now to find your current weather.

    b. Use one of the news searches to find news articles about (*provide current event*).

4. From the *Desk Reference* category:

    a. Find the area code for Jackson, Mississippi _____; Cincinnati, Ohio _____.

    b. Find a quotation from *Bartlett's Quotations* about (*provide the topic*).

5. From the *Other Interesting Searches/Services* category:

    a. Convert the U.S. dollar to Canadian dollar. _____

    b. Locate a recipe for red velvet cake (*or your recipe choice*).

6. Choose a category and determine a search. List category, question, and answer.

8d x and u
Key each line once; repeat.

x Reach *down* with *left third* finger.

u Reach *up* with right first finger.

x

20 x x xs xs ox ox lox sox fox box ex hex lax hex fax
21 sx six sax sox ax fix cox wax hex box pox sex text
22 flax next flex axel pixel exit oxen taxi axis next

u

23 u uj uj jug jut just dust dud due sue use due duel
24 uj us cud but bun out sun nut gun hut hue put fuel
25 dual laud dusk suds fuss full tuna tutus duds full

all reaches learned

26 Paige Power liked the book; Josh can read it next.
27 Next we picked a bag for Jan; then she, Jan, left.
28 Is her June account due? Has Lou ruined her unit?

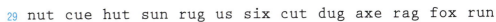

Skillbuilding

8e Reinforcement
Key each line once; DS between groups. Repeat. Print.

29 nut cue hut sun rug us six cut dug axe rag fox run
30 out of the sun|cut the action|a fox den|fun at six
31 That car is not junk; it can run in the next race.

32 etc. tax nick cure lack flex walls uncle clad hurt
33 lack the cash|not just luck|next in line|just once
34 June Dunn can send that next tax case to Rex Knox.

8f Speed Check
1. Key the paragraph. Press ENTER once to begin the second paragraph.
2. Take two 1' writings. Save the timings as **xx8e-t1** and **xx8e-t2**, with *xx* being your initials.

Goal: 14 *wam*.

```
                  .           4           .           8           .
How a finished job will look often depends on how
          12          .          16          .          20
we feel about our work as we do it.  Attitude has
          .          24          .          28          .
a definite effect on the end result of work we do.
```
Press ENTER once
```
                  .           4           .           8           .
When we are eager to begin a job, we relax and do
          12          .          16          .          20
better work than if we start the job with an idea
          .          24          .          28          .
that there is just nothing we can do to escape it.
```

LESSON A | Numeric Keypad

Skillbuilding

Keypad presentation

Keypad instruction is available in the Numeric Keypad module of *Keyboarding Pro* software. NUMLOCK must be on for you to use the software. The lessons are similar to the activities in the other keyboarding modules. Activities include Warmup, Learn New Keys, Improve Keystroking, Build Skill, and a game. The Lesson Report shows the exercises you have completed and the scores achieved.

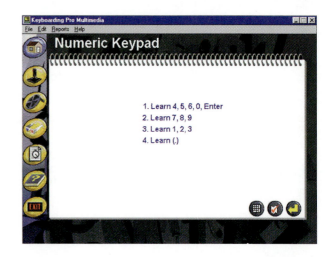

Keypad analysis

Click the **Keypad Analysis** button on the Numeric Keypad Lesson menu for additional keypad practice. You may select from nine different activities (data sets), each of which emphasizes a certain row or number type. Practice is in a timed-writing format.

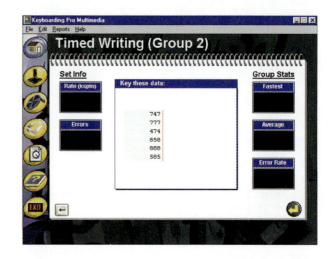

Keypad practice

Click the **Keypad Practice** button to practice the exercises on the next few pages. Strike ENTER on the keypad after each number. Strike enter twice to sum the amounts keyed. Click the **Print** button to print the figures.

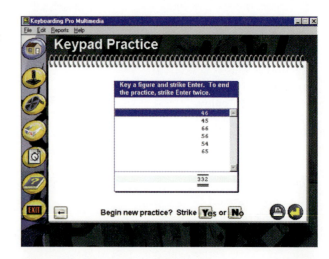

LESSON 8 | G, Question Mark, X, U

Warmup

8a

Key each line twice. Keep eyes on copy.

all 1 Dick will see Job at nine if Rach sees Pat at one.

w/b 2 As the wind blew, Bob Webber saw the window break.

p/, 3 Pat, Pippa, or Cap has prepared the proper papers.

all 4 Bo, Jose, and Will fed Lin; Jack had not paid her.

New Keys

8b **g** and **?**

Key each line once; repeat.

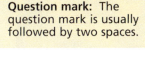

Question mark: The question mark is usually followed by two spaces.

g Reach to *right* with *left first* finger.

? Left SHIFT; reach *down* with *right fourth* finger.

g

5 g g gf gaff gag grog fog frog drag cog dig fig gig

6 gf go gall flag gels slag gala gale glad glee gals

7 golf flog gorge glen high logs gore ogle page grow

?

8 ? ?; ?; ? ? Who? When? Where? Who is? Who was?

9 Who is here? Was it he? Was it she? Did she go?

10 Did Geena? Did he? What is that? Was Jose here?

all reaches learned

11 Has Ginger lost her job? Was her April bill here?

12 Phil did not want the boats to get here this soon.

13 Loris Shin has been ill; Frank, a doctor, saw her.

8c New Key Review

Key each line once; DS between groups.

reach review

14 ws ws hj hj tf tf ol ol rf rf ed ed cd cd bf bf p;

15 wed bid has old hold rid heed heed car bed pot pot

g

16 gf gf gin gin rig ring go gone no nog sign got dog

17 to go|to go|go on|go in|go in|to go in|in the sign

?

18 ?; ?;? who? when? where? how? what? who? It is I?

19 Is she? Is he? Did I lose Jo? Is Gal all right?

TECHNIQUE TIP

Concentrate on correct reaches.

4, 5, 6, 0

1. Turn on NUMLOCK. Click the Keypad Practice button.
2. Strike ENTER after each number.
3. To obtain a total, strike ENTER twice after the last number in a group.
4. Key each problem until the same answer is obtained twice; you can then be reasonably sure that you have the correct answer.

Follow these directions for each lesson.

1 2 3 4

a	b	c	d	e	f
46	55	56	46	55	56
45	64	45	45	64	45
66	56	64	66	56	64
56	44	65	56	44	65
54	65	45	54	65	45
65	54	44	65	54	44

a	b	c	d	e	f
466	445	546	654	465	665
564	654	465	545	446	645
456	464	546	545	564	456
556	544	644	466	644	646
644	455	464	654	464	554
454	546	565	554	456	656

a	b	c	d	e	f
400	404	505	606	500	600
404	505	606	500	600	400
500	600	400	404	505	606
650	506	404	550	440	550
506	460	605	460	604	640
406	500	640	504	460	560

a	b	c	d	e	f
504	640	550	440	660	406
560	450	650	450	505	550
640	504	440	640	450	660
400	600	500	500	600	400
650	505	404	606	540	560
504	404	640	404	406	606

7d Technique Practice

Key each set of lines once SS; DS between 3-line groups.

▼ Space once after a period following an abbreviation.

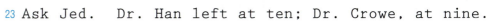

spacing: space *immediately* after each word

20 ad la as in if it lo no of oh he or so ok pi be we

21 an ace ads ale aha a fit oil a jak nor a bit a pew

22 ice ades born is fake to jail than it and the cows

spacing/shifting ▼ ▼

23 Ask Jed. Dr. Han left at ten; Dr. Crowe, at nine.

24 I asked Jin if she had ice in a bowl; it can help.

25 Freda, not Jack, went to Spain. Joan likes Spain.

7e Timed Writings in the Open Screen

STANDARD PLAN [for using the Open Screen Timer]

You can check your speed in the Open Screen using the Timer.

1. In the Open Screen, click the **Timer** button on the toolbar.
   In the Timer dialog box, check **Count-Down Timer** and time; click **OK**.
2. The Timer begins once you start to key and stops automatically. Do not strike ENTER at the end of a line. Wordwrap will cause the text to flow to the next line automatically.
3. To save the timing, click the **File** menu and **Save as**. Use your initals (xx), the exercise number, and number of the timing as the filename. Example: **xx-7f-t1** (your initials, exercise 7f, timing1).
4. Click the **Timer** button again to start a new timing.
5. Each new timing must be saved with its own name.

7f Speed Check

1. Take two 1' writings on the paragraph in the Open Screen.
2. Follow the directions in 7e. Do not strike ENTER at the ends of the lines.

Goal: 12 *wam*.

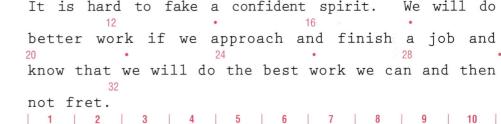

It is hard to fake a confident spirit. We will do better work if we approach and finish a job and know that we will do the best work we can and then not fret.

| 1 | 2 | 3 | 4 | 5 | 6 | 7 | 8 | 9 | 10 |

7g Guided Writing

1. Key each line once for fluency.
2. Set the Timer in the Open Screen for 30". Take two 30" writings on each line. Do not save the timings.

Goal: to reach the end of the line before time is up.

gwam

26 Dan took her to the show. 12

27 Jan lent the bowl to the pros. 14

28 Hold the wrists low for this drill. 16

29 Jessie fit the black panel to the shelf. 18

30 Jake held a bit of cocoa and an apricot for Diane. 20

31 Dick and I fish for cod on the docks at Fish Lake. 20

32 Kent still held the dish and the cork in his hand. 20

| 1 | 2 | 3 | 4 | 5 | 6 | 7 | 8 | 9 | 10 |

D r i l l   2

7, 8, 9

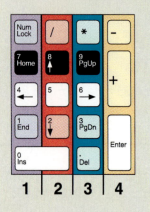

| 1 | 2 | 3 | 4 |

a	b	c	d	e	f
74	85	96	70	80	90
47	58	96	87	78	98
90	70	80	90	90	70
89	98	78	89	77	87
86	67	57	48	68	57
59	47	48	67	58	69

a	b	c	d	e	f
470	580	690	770	707	407
999	969	888	858	474	777
777	474	888	585	999	696

a	b	c	d	e	f
858	969	747	770	880	990
757	858	959	857	747	678
579	849	879	697	854	796
857	967	864	749	864	795
609	507	607	889	990	448
597	847	449	457	684	599

a	b	c	d	e	f
85	74	96	98	78	88
957	478	857	994	677	579
657	947	479	76	94	795
887	965	789	577	649	849
90	80	70	806	709	407
407	567	494	97	80	70

a	b	c	d	e	f
50	790	807	90	75	968
408	97	66	480	857	57
87	479	567	947	808	970
690	85	798	587	907	89
94	754	879	67	594	847
489	880	97	907	69	579

LESSON A   Numeric Keypad

74

LESSON 7 | Review

Warmup

7a
Key each line twice; begin new lines promptly.

all	1	We often can take the older jet to Paris and back.
home	2	a; sl dk fj a;sl dkfj ad as all ask fads adds asks
1st row	3	Ann Bascan and Cabal Naban nabbed a cab in Canada.
3d row	4	Rip went to a water show with either Pippa or Pia.

Skillbuilding

7b Reach Mastery
Key each line once; repeat.

5 ws ws was was wan wan wit wit pew paw nap pop bawl
6 bf bf fb fb fob fob rib rib be be job job bat back
7 p; p; asp asp pan pan ap ap ca cap pa nap pop prow

8 Barb and Bret took an old black robe and the boot.
9 Walt saw a wisp of white water renew ripe peppers.
10 Pat picked a black pepper for the picnic at Parks.

7c Rhythm Builder
Key each line once.

words	11	a an pan so sot la lap ah own do doe el elf to tot
phrases	12	if it|to do|it is|do so|for the|he works|if he bid
sentences	13	Jess ate all of the peas in the salad in the bowl.
words	14	bow bowl pin pint for fork forks hen hens jak jaks
phrases	15	is for|did it|is the|we did a|and so|to see|or not
sentences	16	I hid the ace in a jar as a joke; I do not see it.
words	17	chap chaps flak flake flakes prow prowl work works
phrases	18	as for the|as for the|and to the|to see it|and did
sentences	19	As far as I know, he did not read all of the book.

TECHNIQUE TIP

words: key as a single unit rather than letter by letter;

phrases: say and key fluently;

sentences: work for fluency.

TECHNIQUE TIP

Keep fingers curved and upright over home keys. Keep right thumb tucked under palm.

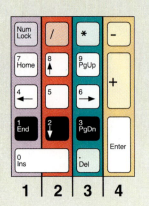

a	b	c	d	e	f
11	22	33	14	15	16
41	52	63	36	34	35
24	26	25	22	42	62
27	18	39	30	20	10
30	30	10	19	61	43
32	31	21	53	83	71

a	b	c	d	e	f
414	141	525	252	636	363
141	111	252	222	363	333
111	414	222	525	333	636

a	b	c	d	e	f
111	141	222	252	366	336
152	342	624	141	243	121
330	502	331	302	110	432
913	823	721	633	523	511
702	612	513	712	802	823
213	293	821	813	422	722

a	b	c	d	e	f
24	36	15	12	32	34
115	334	226	254	346	246
20	140	300	240	105	304
187	278	347	159	357	158
852	741	963	654	321	987
303	505	819	37	92	10

a	b	c	d	e	f
28	91	37	22	13	23
524	631	423	821	922	733
15	221	209	371	300	25
823	421	24	31	19	107
652	813	211	354	231	187
50	31	352	16	210	30

6d b and p
Key each line once.

b Reach *down* with *left first* finger.

p Reach *up* with *right fourth* (little) finger.

b

18 bf bf bf biff fib fib bib bib boa boa fib fibs rob
19 bf bf bf ban ban bon bon bow bow be be rib rib sob
20 a dob, a cob, a crib, a lab, a slab, a bid, a bath

p

21 p; p; pa pa; pal pal pan pan pad par pen pep paper
22 pa pa; lap lap; nap nap; hep ape spa asp leap clap
23 a park, a pan, a pal, a pad, apt to pop, a pair of

all reaches learned

24 Barb and Bob wrapped a pepper in paper and ribbon.
25 Rip, Joann, and Dick were all closer to the flash.
26 Bo will be pleased to see Japan; he works in Oslo.

Skillbuilding

6e Keyboard Reinforcement
Key each line once; key at a steady pace.

reach review
27 ki kid did aid lie hj has has had sw saw wits will
28 de dell led sled jn an en end ant hand k, end, kin

s/w
29 ws ws lows now we shown win cow wow wire jowl when
30 Wes saw an owl in the willow tree in the old lane.

b/p
31 bf bf fib rob bid ;p p; pal pen pot nap hop cap bp
32 Rob has both pans in a bin at the back of the pen.

6f Speed Builder
1. Follow the standard Open Screen directions on page 8.
2. Key each line twice. Work for fluency.

all reaches
33 Dick owns a dock at this lake; he paid Ken for it.
34 Jane also kept a pair of owls, a hen, and a snake.

35 Blair soaks a bit of the corn, as he did in Japan.
36 I blend the cocoa in the bowl when I work for Leo.

37 to do|can do|to bow|ask her|to nap|to work|is born
38 for this|if she|is now|did all|to see|or not|or if

LESSON B | Word Processing

New Functions

Overview of Open Screen

At almost any time while using *Keyboarding Pro*, you can access the Open Screen feature by clicking the Open Screen button. You can use the Open Screen word processor to practice your keyboarding skill, create a letter, or take a timed writing.

The word processor has several formatting and editing features, including margins, tabs, justification, line spacing, bold, italic, undo, find and replace, and page numbers. These and other commands are available from the menu bar at the top of the screen (File, Edit, Format, and Style) as well as the toolbar. (See page xi for an illustration.)

Commands

A pull-down menu displays when you click on a name in the **menu bar**. Each menu contains commands. Commands may be selected by clicking the menu name with the mouse and then clicking the command. An ellipsis (. . .) following a command indicates that a dialog box will display. If a command is unavailable, it appears dimmed.

The **toolbar** provides a quick way to use common features such as bold. The screen also has buttons for changing tabs, aligning text, or changing the line spacing. You will learn to use the Help menu to use these and other features.

Dialog Box

A **dialog box** displays when the system needs more information to carry out the task. Menu items that are followed by ellipsis (. . .) will open a dialog box. Items that are dimmed are not available at this point. Figure 1 displays many of the common elements of a dialog box.

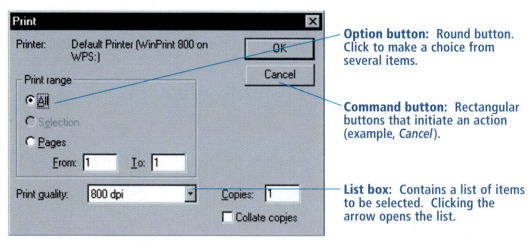

Option button: Round button. Click to make a choice from several items.

Command button: Rectangular buttons that initiate an action (example, *Cancel*).

List box: Contains a list of items to be selected. Clicking the arrow opens the list.

Figure 1: Dialog box options

LESSON 6 | W, Comma, B, P

Warmup

6a

Key each line twice; avoid pauses.

home row 1 ask a lad; a fall fad; had a salad; ask a sad jak;

o/t 2 to do it; to toil; as a tot; do a lot; he told her

c/r 3 cots are; has rocks; roll cot; is rich; has an arc

all reaches 4 Holt can see Dane at ten; Jill sees Frank at nine.

New Keys

6b w and , (comma)

Key each line once.

Comma: Space once after a comma.

w Reach *up* with *left third* finger.

, (comma) Reach *down* with *right second* finger.

w

5 w ws ws was was wan wit low win jaw wilt wink wolf

6 sw sw ws ow ow now now row row own own wow wow owe

7 to sew; to own; was rich; was in; is how; will now

, (comma)

8 k, k, k, irk, ilk, ask, oak, ark, lark, jak, rock,

9 skis, a dock, a fork, a lock, a fee, a tie, a fan,

10 Jo, Ed, Ted, and Dan saw Nan in a car lift; a kit

all reaches learned

11 Win, Lew, Drew, and Walt will walk to West Willow.

12 Ask Ho, Al, and Jared to read the code; it is new.

13 The window, we think, was closed; we felt no wind.

6c New Key Mastery

Key each line twice; DS between groups.

14 walk wide sown wild town went jowl wait white down

15 a dock, a kit, a wick, a lock, a row, a cow, a fee

16 Joe lost to Ron; Fiji lost to Cara; Don lost to Al

17 Kane will win; Nan will win; Rio will win; Di wins

18 Walter is in Reno; Tia is in Tahoe; then to Hawaii

Help

Keyboarding Pro provides help without your having to look up answers in a documentation manual. Let's use Help to become familiar with the software.

Drill 1

1. Click **File** in the menu bar. Observe the items in the File menu.
2. Click **Open** to display the Open dialog box.
3. From the Open dialog box, click **Cancel** to close the dialog box.
4. Click **Edit** to view the items in the Edit menu.
5. Click to view the Format and Style menus.

Drill 2

1. From the menu bar, click **Help**, then **Contents**. Under "Getting Started," click **Navigating the Software**, then **Open Screen**.
2. Scroll through the information using the scroll bar.
3. On the menu bar, click **File** and then **Print Topic** to print.

Drill 3

1. From the menu bar, click **Help**, then **Contents**. Under "Using Special Features," click **Open Screen**.
2. Choose *Open/Saving a Document*.

Drill 4

1. Key the paragraph.
2. Click the **Save** button. Key **drill-4** in the Filename box.
3. Click **New** button. You now have a clear screen.
4. Click **Open** button. Click **drill-4** then **OK** to open Drill 4.
5. Position the insertion point at the beginning of Sentence 2. Press **enter**. You now have 3 ¶s.
6. Continue to Drill 5. Do not exit this document.

Serendipity, a new homework research tool from Information Technology Company, is available to subscribers of the major online services via the World Wide Web. Offered as a subscription service aimed at college students, Serendipity is a collection of tens of thousands of articles from major encyclopedias, reference books, magazines, pamphlets, and Internet sources combined into a single searchable database.

Serendipity puts an electronic library right at students' fingertips. The program offers two browse-and-search capabilities. Users can find articles by entering questions in simple question format or browse the database by pointing and clicking on key words that identify related articles. For more information, call 800-555-4374 or address e-mail to <<lab@serendipity.com>>.

5d c and o
Key each line once.

c Reach *down* with *left second* finger.

o Reach *up* with right *third finger*.

c

20 c c cd cd cad cad can can tic ice sac cake cat sic
21 clad chic cite cheek clef sick lick kick dice rice
22 call acid hack jack lack lick cask crack clan cane

o

23 o ol ol old old of off odd ode or ore oar soar one
24 ol sol sold told dole do doe lo doll sol solo odor
25 onto door toil lotto soak fort hods foal roan load

all reaches learned

26 Carlo Rand can call Rocco; Cole can call Doc Cost.
27 Trina can ask Dina if Nick Corl has left; Joe did.
28 Case sent Carole a nice skirt; it fits Lorna Rich.

Skillbuilding

5e Keyboard Reinforcement
Key each line once SS; key at a steady pace. Repeat, striving for control.

TECHNIQUE TIP

Reach up without moving hands away from your body. Use quick keystrokes.

o/r
29 or or for for nor nor ore ore oar oar roe roe sore
30 a rose|her or|he or|he rode|or for|a door|her doll

i/t
31 is is tis tis it it fit fit tie tie this this lits
32 it is|it is|it is this|it is this|it sits|tie fits

e/n
33 en en end end ne ne need need ken ken kneel kneels
34 lend the|lend the|at the end|at the end|need their

c/o
35 ch ch check check ck ck hack lack jack co co cones
36 the cot|the cot|a dock|a dock|a jack|a jack|a cone

all reaches
37 Jack and Rona did frost nine of the cakes at last.
38 Jo can ice her drink if Tess can find her a flask.
39 Ask Jean to call Fisk at noon; he needs her notes.

Insert/Delete

Insert and Delete features are used to correct errors or revise documents.

Insert: To insert text, simply position the insertion point at the location where the new text is to appear and key the text. Existing text moves to the right.

Delete: The DELETE key erases text that is no longer needed.

To delete a character: Position the insertion point to the left of the character to delete and press DELETE or position the insertion point to the right of the character to delete and press BACKSPACE. Be careful not to hold down the delete or backspace keys since they will continue to erase characters.

To delete a word: Double-click the word to be deleted and press DELETE.

Select

Select identifies text that has been keyed so that it can be modified. Selected text appears black on the screen. Select text using the mouse.

To select text	Position the insertion point on the first character to be selected. Click the left mouse button and drag the mouse over the text to be selected. To cancel select, click the mouse again.
To select a word	Double-click the word.
To select a paragraph	Triple-click in the paragraph.
To select multiple lines	Click the left mouse button and drag in the area left of the lines.

D r i l l 5

1. Make the deletions shown at the right. (Your document will be single-spaced.)

2. Correct any other errors you may have made.

3. Save as **drill-5**.

4. Click the **Print** button on the toolbar.

5. Do not exit Drill 5; go on to Drill 6.

Serendipity, a ~~new homework~~ research tool from Information Technology Company, is available to subscribers of ~~the major~~ on-line services via the World Wide Web.

Offered as a subscription service aimed at ~~college~~ students, Serendipity is a collection of tens of thousands of articles from ~~major~~ encyclopedias, reference books, magazines, pamphlets, and Internet sources combined into a single searchable database.

Serendipity puts an electronic library right at students' fingertips. The program offers two browse-and-search capabilities. Users can find articles *on just about any subject* by entering questions in simple question format or browse the database by pointing and clicking on key words that identify related articles. For more information, call 800-555-4374 or address e-mail to <<lab@serendipity.com>>. *with just a computer and a modem.*

LESSON 5 | R, Right Shift, C, O

Warmup

5a
Key each line twice.

home keys 1 a; ad add al all lad fad jak ask lass fall jak lad
t/h/i/n 2 the hit tin nit then this kith dint tine hint thin
left shift/. 3 I need ink. Li has an idea. Hit it. I see Kate.
all reaches 4 Jeff ate at ten; he left a salad dish in the sink.

New Keys

5b r and Right Shift
Key each line once.

r Reach *up* with *left first* finger.

right shift Reach *down* with *right fourth* finger; shift, strike, release.

5c New Key Mastery
Key each line twice. DS between groups.

r

5 r rf rf riff riff fir fir rid ire jar air sir lair
6 rf rid ark ran rat are hare art rant tire dirt jar
7 rare dirk ajar lark rain kirk share hart rail tart

right shift

8 D D Dan Dan Dale Ti Sal Ted Ann Ed Alf Ada Sid Fan
9 and Sid and Dina and Allen and Eli and Dean and Ed
10 Ed Dana; Dee Falk; Tina Finn; Sal Alan; Anna Deeds

all reaches learned

11 Jane and Ann hiked in the sand; Asa set the tents.
12 a rake; a jar; a tree; a red fire; a fare; a rain;
13 Fred Derr and Rai Tira dined at the Tree Art Fair.

14 ir ir ire fir first air fair fire tire rid sir
15 fir jar tar fir flit rill till list stir dirt fire

16 Feral is ill. Dan reads. Dee and Ed Finn see Dere.
17 All is still as Sarah and I fish here in the rain.

18 I still see a red ash tree that fell in the field.
19 Lana said she did sail her skiff in the dark lake.

Drill 6

1. The document, drill-5, that you keyed earlier should be open. If not, open the document. Use the mouse to select each of the following items. Select cancel after each item.
   - The first sentence.
   - The word Serendipity in ¶ 1.
   - All of ¶ 1.
   - The entire document.

2. Move the insertion point to the beginning of the document. Press enter 4 times. Key your name at the left margin. Do not save or print.

Bold, Italic, Underline, Fonts

 Sometimes you may want to emphasize or enhance the appearance of text by adding bold, underline, or italic. The size of the characters can also be changed for added emphasis.

To apply formats as you key: Click the appropriate button and key the text. Click the same button again to turn off the format.

To apply formats to text that has already been keyed: Select the text and then click the appropriate button.

To change the font style or size, click **Format** on the menu bar and then **Character Format**. Make your selection.

Justification/Alignment

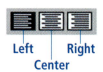
Left   Right
Center

Text can be aligned or justified at the left, right, or center. To justify text, click the desired button. To justify existing text, select the text and then apply justification.

Line Spacing

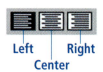
SS   1.5   2

Line spacing may be single, one and a half, or double. To change the line spacing, click the appropriate button. All paragraphs following the command will be affected.

To change the spacing of a paragraph that has already been keyed, position the insertion point in the paragraph and change the line spacing. To change several paragraphs, select the text first.

Drill 7

Key each of the sentences, applying the format as you key. Save as **drill-7**. Print. .

Clear the screen (click **New** button).

1. **These words are keyed in bold.**

2. *These words are keyed in italic.*

3. <u>These words are underlined</u>.

4. This line is keyed in 14 point.

4d `t` and `.` (period)
Key each line once.

t Reach *up* with *left first* finger.

. (period) Reach *down* with *right third* finger.

Period: Space once after a period that follows an initial or an abbreviation. To increase readability, space twice after a period that ends a sentence.

LEFT FINGERS 4 \ 3 \ 2 \ 1 \ 1 \ 2 \ 3 \ 4 RIGHT FINGERS

t

18 t tf tf aft aft left fit fat fete tiff tie the tin

19 tf at at aft lit hit tide tilt tint sits skit this

20 hat kit let lit ate sit flat tilt thin tale tan at

. (period)

21 .l .l l.l fl. fl. L. L. Neal and J. N. List hiked.

22 Hand J. H. Kass a fan. Jess did. I need an idea.

23 Jane said she has a tan dish; Jae and Lee need it.

all reaches learned

24 I did tell J. K. that Lt. Li had left. He is ill.

25 tie tan kit sit fit hit hat; the jet left at nine.

26 I see Lila and Ilene at tea. Jan Kane ate at ten.

Skillbuilding

4e Reinforcement

Lines 27–34: Key each line twice in the Open Screen. Try to increase your speed the second time.

Lines 35–38: Key the lines once; repeat.

reach review

27 tf .l hj ft ki de jh tf ik ed hj de ft ki l. tf ik

28 elf eel left is sis fit till dens ink has delt ink

h/e

29 he he heed heed she she shelf shelf shed shed she

30 he has; he had; he led; he sleds; she fell; he is

i/t

31 it is if id did lit tide tide tile tile list list

32 it is; he hit it; he is ill; she is still; she is

shift

33 Hal and Nel; Jade dishes; Kale has half; Jed hides

34 Hi Ken; Helen and Jen hike; Jan has a jade; Ken is

enter

35 Nan had a sale.

36 He did see Hal.

37 Lee has a desk.

38 Ina hid a dish.

TECHNIQUE TIP

Strike `Enter` without pausing or looking up from the copy.

End the lesson

Print the lines keyed in the Open Screen and print your Lesson Report. Exit the software.

Drill 8

FORMATS, LINE SPACING, FONTS

1. Key the text without the character formats.
2. Save as **drill-8**.
3. Select the appropriate text and apply the formats as shown.
4. Select THE INTERNET and apply 14 point.
5. Save **drill-8** again and print. Do not close the document.
6. Place the insertion point in ¶ 1. Click **1.5** spacing.
7. Place the insertion point in ¶ 2. Click **2** for double spacing.
8. Save as **drill-8r** and print.

THE INTERNET

The **Internet** is a *web* of wide-area networks that allows you to connect with computers all over the world. Most major universities, science research centers, government agencies, and technology-oriented businesses have linked their networks to the **Internet** to exchange electronic information.

If your school is connected to the **Internet**, you can send *e-mail* to most major universities throughout the world. Messages delivered through the **Internet** can take anywhere from two minutes to six hours.

Drill 9

FORMATS, CENTER PAGE

1. Key the text applying the formats shown.
2. Center the page: On the menu bar, click Format, then Page Settings. Click in the Center Page box to add a check mark. Click Apply.
3. Save as drill-9; print.

THE INTERNET

Full Align → The Internet is the greatest entertainment medium since television and the greatest business tool since the computer. Don't be left wondering; cruise the Internet and find out for yourself.

Left Align → Each time you browse, you will find different places and different information. Here are a few of the benefits the Internet offers you:

Center Align → Interactive entertainment
A chance to meet people on the Net
Research sites
Business opportunities

Left Align → Even if you don't like computers, the Internet will be the catalyst that brings you into the computer age.

Right Align → For more information or help, contact:
THE INTERNET HELP DESK
301 Web Avenue
Seattle, WA 98543-3276

Left Align → Your Name

LESSON 4 | Left Shift, H, T, Period

 W a r m u p

4a
Key each line twice SS.
Keep eyes on copy.

home row	1	al as ads lad dad fad jak fall lass asks fads all;
e/i/n	2	ed ik jn in knee end nine line sine lien dies leis
all reaches	3	see a ski; add ink; fed a jak; is an inn; as a lad
easy	4	an dial id is an la lake did el ale fake is land a

New Keys

4b Left [Shift] and [h]
Key each line once.

Follow the "Standard procedures for learning new keyreaches" on p. 4 for all remaining reaches.

left shift Reach *down* with *left fourth* (little) finger; shift, strike, release.

left shift

5 J Ja Ja Jan Jan Jane Jana Ken Kass Lee Len Nan Ned
6 and Ken and Lena and Jake and Lida and Nan and Ida
7 Inn is; Jill Ina is; Nels is; Jen is; Ken Lin is a

h

8 h hj hj he he she she hen aha ash had has hid shed
9 h hj ha hie his half hand hike dash head sash shad
10 aha hi hash heal hill hind lash hash hake dish ash

h Reach to *left* with *right first* finger.

all reaches learned

11 Nels Kane and Jake Jenn; she asked Hi and Ina Linn
12 Lend Lana and Jed a dish; I fed Lane and Jess Kane
13 I see Jake Kish and Lash Hess; Isla and Helen hike

4c New Key Mastery
Key the drill once; DS and repeat. Strive for good control.

14 he she held a lead; she sells jade; she has a sale
15 Ha Ja Ka La Ha Hal Ja Jake Ka Kahn La Ladd Ha Hall
16 Hal leads; Jeff led all fall; Hal has a safe lead
17 Hal Hall heads all sales; Jake Hess asks less fee;

Document Design

Business Letter Guides

Business Letters

Business letters are used to communicate with persons outside of the business. Business letters carry two messages: one is the tone and content; a second is the appearance of the document. Appearance is important because it creates the critical first impression. Stationery, use of standard letter parts, and placement should convey that the writer is intelligent, informed, and detail minded.

Stationery

Letters should be printed on high-quality (about 24-pound) letterhead stationery. Standard size for letterhead is $8\frac{1}{2}$" x 11". Envelopes should match the letterhead in quality and color.

Letter parts

Businesspeople expect to see standard letter parts arranged in the proper sequence. The standard parts are listed below. Other letter parts may be included as needed.

Letterhead: Preprinted stationery that includes the company name, logo, address, and other optional information such as a telephone number and fax number.

Dateline: Date the letter is prepared.

Letter address: Complete address of the person who will receive the letter. Generally, the address includes the receiver's name, company name, street address, city, state (followed by one space only), and ZIP code. Include a personal title (*Mr.*, *Ms.*, *Dr.*) with the person's name. Key the address four lines below the dateline, and capitalize the first letter of each word.

Salutation: Key the salutation, or greeting, a double space (DS) below the letter address. If the letter is addressed to an individual, include a courtesy title with the person's last name. If the letter is addressed to a company, use *Ladies and Gentlemen*.

Body: Begin the body, or message, a DS below the salutation. Single-space (SS) paragraphs and DS between paragraphs.

Complimentary closing: Begin the complimentary closing a DS below the body. Capitalize only the first letter of the closing.

Writer's name and title: Key the writer's name and job title four lines below the complimentary closing to allow space for the writer's signature. Key the name and title on either one or two lines, whichever gives better balance to the signature block. Separate the writer's name and title with a comma if they are on one line.

Reference initials: Key the initials of the typist in lowercase letters a DS below the typed name and title. If the writer's initials are also included, key them first in ALL CAPS followed by a colon (BB:xx).

Block Letter

Envelope

Block Format

In block format, all letter parts are keyed at the left margin. For most letters, use open punctuation, which requires no punctuation after the salutation or the closing. For efficiency, use the default settings and features of your software when formatting letters.

Side margins: Default (1.25") or 1"

Dateline: About 2" (strike ENTER six times), center the page vertically, or at least 0.5" below the letterhead. If the letter is short, center the page vertically.

Spacing: SS paragraphs; DS between them. Follow the directions for spacing between other letter parts provided above.

3d Keyboard Mastery

Key each line once;
repeat drill.

LEFT FINGERS 4 \ 3 \ 2 \ 1 \ 1 \ 2 \ 3 \ 4 RIGHT FINGERS

TECHNIQUE TIP

Strike keys quickly.
Strike the Space Bar with down-and-in motion.
Strike Enter with a quick flick of the little finger.

reach review

19 ea sea lea seas deal leaf leak lead leas fleas keas

20 as ask lass ease as asks ask ask sass as alas seas

21 sa sad sane sake sail sale sans safe sad said sand

22 le sled lead flee fled ale flea lei dale kale leaf

23 jn jn nj nj in fan fin an; din ink sin and inn an;

24 de den end fen an an and and ken knee nee dean dee

phrases (think and key phrases)

25 and and land land el el elf elf self self ail nail

26 as as ask ask ad ad lad lad id id lid lid kid kids

27 if if|is is|jak jak|all all|did did|nan nan|elf elf

28 as a lad| ask dad| fed a jak| as all ask| sales fad

29 sell a lead|seal a deal|feel a leaf|if a jade sale

30 is a |is as if|a disk|aid all kids|did ski|is a silk

3e Reinforcement

1. In the Open Screen, key your name. Insert a hard return.
2. Key each line once. DS between groups of two lines.
3. Print the exercise.
4. Click the X box in the upper-right corner to close the Open Screen.
5. Print your Lesson Report and Exit.

d/e

31 den end fen ken dean dens ales fend fens keen knee

32 a deed; a desk; a jade; an eel; a jade eel; a dean

n/a

33 an an in in and and en end end sane sane sand sand

34 a land; a dean; a fan; a fin; a sane end; end land

nj

35 el eel eld elf sell self el dell fell elk els jell

36 in fin inn inks dine sink fine fins kind line lain

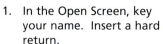
all reaches

37 an and fan dean elan flan land lane lean sand sane

38 sell a lead; sell a jade; seal a deal; feel a leaf

Finger Gymnastics

Brief daily practice of finger gymnastics will strengthen your finger muscles and increase the ease with which you key. Begin each keying period with this conditioning exercise. Choose two or more drills for this practice.

DRILL 1. Hands open, fingers wide, muscles tense. Close the fingers into a tight "fist," with thumb on top. Relax the fingers as you straighten them; repeat 10 times.

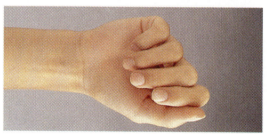

DRILL 2. Clench the fingers as shown. Hold the fingers in this position for a brief time; then extend the fingers, relaxing the muscles of fingers and hand. Repeat the movements slowly several times. Exercise both hands at the same time.

DRILL 3. Place the fingers and the thumb of one hand between two fingers of the other hand, and spread the fingers as much as possible. Spread all fingers of both hands.

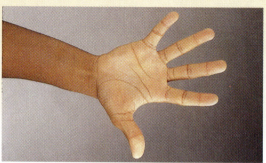

DRILL 4. Interlace the fingers of the two hands and wring the hands, rubbing the heel of the palms vigorously.

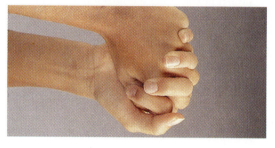

DRILL 5. Spread the fingers as much as possible, holding the position for a moment or two; then relax the fingers and lightly fold them into the palm of the hand. Repeat the movements slowly several times. Exercise both hands at the same time.

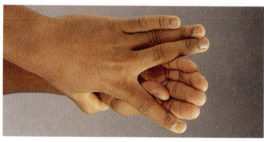

DRILL 6. Rub the hands vigorously. Let the thumb rub the palm of the hand. Rub the fingers, the back of the hand, and the wrist.

DRILL 7. Hold both hands in front of you, fingers together. Hold the last three fingers still and move the first finger as far to the side as possible. Return the first finger; then move the first and second fingers together; finally move the little finger as far to the side as possible.

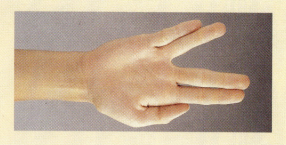